FAITHFUL FUTURES

SACRED TOOLS FOR ENGAGING YOUNGER GENERATIONS

JOSH PACKARD

Baker Academic
a division of Baker Publishing Group
Grand Rapids, Michigan

© 2025 by Josh Packard

Published by Baker Academic
a division of Baker Publishing Group
Grand Rapids, Michigan
BakerAcademic.com

All rights reserved. No part of this publication may be reproduced, stored in a retrieval system, or transmitted in any form or by any means—for example, electronic, photocopy, recording—without the prior written permission of the publisher. The only exception is brief quotations in printed reviews.

Library of Congress Cataloging-in-Publication Data
Names: Packard, Josh author
Title: Faithful futures : sacred tools for engaging younger generations / Josh Packard.
Description: Grand Rapids, Michigan : Baker Academic, a division of Baker Publishing Group, [2025] | Includes bibliographical references and index.
Identifiers: LCCN 2025005501 | ISBN 9781540969514 paperback | ISBN 9781540969620 casebound | ISBN 9781493451906 ebook | ISBN 9781493451913 pdf
Subjects: LCSH: Church work with youth—United States | Christian leadership—United States | Generation Z—Miscellanea | Generation Alpha—Miscellanea
Classification: LCC BV4447 .P236 2025 | DDC 259/.23—dc23/eng/20250512
LC record available at https://lccn.loc.gov/2025005501

Some names and details of the people and situations described in this book have been changed or presented in composite form to ensure the privacy of those with whom the author has worked.

Emojis are from the open-source library OpenMoji (https://openmoji.org/) under the Creative Commons license CC BY-SA 4.0 (https://creativecommons.org/licenses/by-sa/4.0/legalcode).

Baker Publishing Group publications use paper produced from sustainable forestry practices and postconsumer waste whenever possible.

25 26 27 28 29 30 31   7 6 5 4 3 2 1

To young people everywhere
and the adults who care about them.
You are more important than you know.

CONTENTS

Acknowledgments   ix

Introduction   1

1. Gen Z and Gen Alpha   19
2. Faith Is a Conversation   57
3. A Disaffiliated World   81
4. Belonging Precedes Believing   111
5. The COVID Effect   137
6. Growing Up Online   163
7. Micronarratives   189

Index   197

ACKNOWLEDGMENTS

First and foremost, I wish to thank my wife, Megan, and my son, Holden, for their unwavering support, time, and invaluable insights. Their presence and patience have been a grounding force throughout this journey.

My deep gratitude goes to my cofounder at Future of Faith, Megan Bissell, whose dedication, brilliance, and tireless work helped bring Sacred Listening to life. Her commitment to the research and to shaping this project has been instrumental.

I am equally grateful to the countless youth ministers, pastors, religious professionals, and others who generously shared their time, thoughts, and stories with me. Each conversation has been a reminder of the commitment and passion these leaders bring to their work and of how much we all gain when we listen deeply.

To the team at Baker, I owe immense thanks for your enthusiasm, expert guidance, and willingness to see this project through. Your immediate belief in this book's potential has made this process a rewarding endeavor. Thanks, Terry, for the introduction.

Finally, I extend a heartfelt thanks to the young people who have shared their lives with me over the years. Whether through research responses or thoughtful conversations about faith, your openness has provided essential insights into the changing landscape of belief. This book carries your voices within its pages, and I am honored to be able to amplify them here.

INTRODUCTION

Call Pinaki

When I was in graduate school, my friend and classmate got engaged. Mostly out of politeness, she extended an invitation to her wedding to everyone in her cohort. I say "politeness" because I don't imagine she expected us to actually show up. My friend is from India, her wedding was to be in Calcutta, and we were all very poor graduate students—is there any other kind? We simply had no business flying around the world for a wedding.

But then again, when were we ever going to get the opportunity to experience an authentic Indian wedding? My wife and I didn't even really think about it much before deciding we were going—regardless of the cost. It took a while to convince my friend that we were actually going to show up, during which time I'm quite certain she regretted even inviting us in the first place.

When she finally accepted that our flights were booked and we were definitely coming, she said, "OK. Fine. But please, while you're there, take my family's driver, Pinaki." I looked at her incredulously and indicated there was no way we were commandeering her family driver during the week of her wedding just so we—some borderline wedding crashers—could be chauffeured around. I was willing to impose, but only to an extent.

"But how will you get around if you don't have a driver?" she asked.

"It'll be fine," I said. "I'm from Dallas."

Well, friends, we were there for about eight hours before we realized we were in *way* over our heads. We were lost beyond words. Everything was a struggle. It took ten times longer than it should to get from one place to another. Things that should have been simple were impossible. We couldn't find a grocery store or basic landmarks. And if we did manage to get out of our neighborhood, we had precious little chance of finding our way back directly. It was unlike any driving or navigating experience I had ever had.

So we called and asked for Pinaki, and it made all the difference in the world.

My belief that I could navigate Calcutta on the basis of my experiences driving around Dallas was understandable—and wildly incorrect. Our brains have evolved to do some things very, very well to help ensure our survival. One of those things, as well documented by social psychologists and neuroscientists over the last fifty years, is how we deal with novel situations.[1] Basically, we look at something that is new, quickly assess what we have done or experienced that is most similar, and reason from our experience of one thing to help us navigate the other. We look for information that is available and certain so we can bring some predictability to a situation that is otherwise uncertain.

This ability is one of the most fundamental components of being human. We don't have to learn each unique situation. We can use our past experiences to make sense of things we've never seen. Scientists call it pattern recognition.[2]

Pattern recognition allows us to extract meaning, identify potential threats or opportunities, and adapt our behavior accordingly. Our ancestors relied on this cognitive process to navigate the complexities of their environments, identify edible plants,

---

1. Daniel Kahneman, *Thinking, Fast and Slow* (Farrar, Straus and Giroux, 2011).
2. Christopher Chabris and Daniel Simons, *The Invisible Gorilla: And Other Ways Our Intuitions Deceive Us* (Crown, 2010).

recognize dangerous predators, and form social bonds with fellow humans.

This is basically what I was doing. Calcutta, I reasoned, is a large city. Dallas is also a large city. Throw in a healthy dash of Texas pride, and it's easy to see why I thought I could use one to navigate the other: pattern recognition.

But the truth is that Calcutta is a wholly different kind of thing than Dallas. They are both cities by definition, but in practice, very little is the same. And so pattern recognition actually worked against me.

We've been making this same kind of mistake when we think about Gen Z and Gen Alpha. We keep trying to understand them by relying on what is available and certain. Most of us go back to our own teenage years to try and understand today's teenagers. This is what people in ministry positions have done for years, and for a very long time it worked pretty well. We were essentially translating from driving around Dallas to driving around Kansas City. Not so different.

But now, we find ourselves in Calcutta. The experiences of Gens Z and Alpha are so different from our own that our mental models and maps are essentially useless. The more we try to rely on what life was like for us as teenagers, the more we find ourselves helplessly out of touch. And the more we try to use the tools that adults used to reach us as teens, the more we struggle to make any kind of connection.

Echoing the wisdom of a quote mistakenly ascribed to Mark Twain, "It ain't what you don't know that gets you into trouble. It's what you know for sure that just ain't so," we confront a stark truth. Believing that the essence of being a teenager is a universal experience that transcends time leads us into pitfalls. The more we use the lens of our own teenage years to understand Generations Z and Alpha, the more we falter.

What we need is a way to bust out of this trap. We need a guide. We need Pinaki.

It's my hope that this book can be your Pinaki, your guide to these new and incredibly exciting generations. Throughout the chapters, I'll be relying on fresh data and innovative practices that engage young people, as well as sound social science, to help frame and understand these generations and ultimately equip you to reach them no matter what environment you're in.

This Book

In the first chapter, I offer some broad definitions of our newest generations, Gen Z and Gen Alpha, and suggest a novel way to think about these incredible generations. The next three chapters focus on the enduring social trends that are shaping these young people and, to some extent, the generations before them. Chapters 5 and 6 focus on the defining moments that make today's teenagers unique and require us to respond to them differently than we have ever responded to any young people. The final chapter offers the idea of micronarratives to help better understand young people. Along the way, I'll be sharing some of the most effective practices I've come across for engaging these generations after years of research.

In chapter 2, I take a look at how the "project" of faith has shifted for these generations. Emerging generations experience faith as a conversation rather than a static state of being. They have made it clear that they are not going to simply take a pre-packaged set of beliefs and ideas about religion or spirituality and adopt them as their own. On the one hand, this can be frustrating for those of us who have so much invested in those systems. Gone are the days when we can simply get young people plugged into a youth group or confirmation class and expect that they will walk out with a robust faith to last a lifetime. However, there is also an opportunity to build deeper, longer-lasting, and more vibrant spiritual lives in young people if we can take the time to engage them in critical conversations throughout their faith journey.

Chapter 3 explores the importance of building the right relational tools for our world. Right now, many of the tools that we have built for ministry rely on an assumption of trust. We assume that parents and young people trust churches, religious institutions, and religious leaders. In a world where that trust exists, we work to get young people more connected and integrated into the institution itself. Primarily working through programs, we try to get them into the building more often and center interactions on the institution's agenda. For example, my own confirmation experience was directed by a curriculum handed down from the denomination that we "had" to make it through (regardless of how many questions we asked!).

Programs, curricula, and time in the building are all effective tools to nurture faith and spiritual development in a high-trust world. But we don't live in that world anymore. Study after study has shown that we are living in a time of eroding institutional trust. Levels of trust in organizations, leaders, and one another are at or near all-time lows. The same tools that worked in a high-trust world are not likely to be very effective now. This chapter will show why relational authority is the low-trust tool we need to have a real impact and influence in the life of a young person today.

In chapter 4, I explain how we often get the relationship between belonging and believing backward and why it's more crucial now than ever to understand this fundamental dynamic. Our young people are living through times of unprecedented loneliness and isolation. We can help them and strengthen our ministries by understanding that belonging precedes believing, not the other way around. If we can take some simple steps to help young people connect to us, one another, and their surrounding communities, ministry opportunities will arise naturally and lead to a faith life that can withstand life's ups and downs.

Finally, two defining historical events have profoundly influenced Generations Z and Alpha: COVID and the rise of social media. In chapter 5, I take a deep look at the impact of the COVID-19 pandemic on these emerging generations. In particular, the pandemic has made dramatic alterations to faith formation opportunities for young people. Additionally, the mental health consequences of the pandemic are substantial and long-lasting. The pandemic and its aftereffects are defining features of these emerging generations' lives and calls to action for religious leaders to respond to these unique needs.

Chapter 6 shows what social media is really doing to young people and what its implications are for their faith lives. We are only just now beginning to get conclusive data about the effect of social media on the development of teenagers. In this chapter, I couple this emerging data with core scientific lessons to help leaders make sense of how these new and emerging technologies are affecting young people at a neurological and social level, so we can all assess and respond in ways that will strengthen and nurture opportunities for faith formation.

Chapter 7 concludes by challenging the assumption that young people today reject truth and authority altogether. It explores their pursuit of *micronarratives*—personal, integrated worldviews that reconcile ancient traditions with modern realities. By adopting the Sacred Listening tools outlined throughout this book, you can help young people navigate their questions, build trust, and cocreate vibrant faith journeys that foster meaningful connections and revitalize communities.

Sacred Listening Theory

The need for Pinaki's guidance through the streets of Calcutta wasn't just about knowing where to go. It was about understanding how the city worked, how to navigate the complexities we couldn't see, and how to adapt as the environment shifted around us. It's easy to think that we can lead ministries by relying on familiar tools and past experiences, but that's where the mistake lies. We need something deeper—something rooted not just in practice but in the sacredness of relationships.

At the heart of every ministry, every community, and every relationship is listening. Real listening. But this is not the kind of listening where you nod along, waiting for your turn to speak. This is listening with intention. It's the kind of listening that starts with the understanding that each person we encounter is created in the image of the divine. It's listening that seeks to uncover the sacred in every interaction. This is the foundation of Sacred Listening theory.

In my years of research and work with emerging generations, one truth stands out: If we want to reach young people today, we have to get better at listening to them. And not just listening to their words but understanding their lives, their struggles, and the context that shapes them. In 2024 Future of Faith conducted a nationally representative survey of over 1,100 teenagers about the importance of listening, and the results were stunning:

- 71 percent of teenagers said that they experience deeper faith when they feel heard.
- 74 percent agreed that when someone listens without judgment, they feel more connected to that person.
- 73 percent said that when they feel listened to in a conversation about faith or spirituality, it makes them more likely to be open about those topics in the future.
- 75 percent indicated that being listened to helps them process spiritual challenges like doubt, disillusionment, and grief.[3]

Being listened to was also strongly associated with feelings of self-efficacy, reducing loneliness, and relieving stress. Given all of this, it would not be a stretch to conclude that listening is the most important work an adult can do for a young person.

But listening is no easy task. It's not enough to have coffee with a few kids and call it a day. If we want to engage with dozens, hundreds, or even thousands of young people, we need a way to scale relationships while maintaining the depth and intentionality that true ministry requires. That's where Sacred Listening comes in.

Sacred Listening theory draws from three areas of thought—theology, communication theory, and sociology—to create a model of listening that's both scalable and deeply personal. Each of these fields offers essential insights, but it's the combination

3. Future of Faith, *Sacred Listening, Deeper Faith: A Research-Driven Approach* (Future of Faith, 2025), https://www.futureoffaith.org/sacredlisteningstudy.

that makes Sacred Listening more than just a theory. It's a practice that anyone in ministry can use to build trust, foster deeper relationships, and honor the people they serve.

Imago Dei: Recognizing the Divine in Every Person

The first element of Sacred Listening theory is theology, specifically the concept of *imago Dei*—the belief that every person is made in the image of God. This is not just a theological statement; it's a guiding principle for how we should approach every conversation. When we truly believe that the person sitting across from us reflects the divine, we listen differently. We approach the conversation with reverence, understanding that the moment is not ordinary. It's sacred.

Setting an intention is the first step in Sacred Listening. Before any interaction, we pause and recognize the holiness of the moment. Whether this intention is spoken aloud, written down, or simply held in the heart, it shapes the way we engage. We're not just passing time or exchanging pleasantries. We're encountering the sacred in another person. When ministry leaders embrace this posture, it changes everything. Conversations move from superficial to meaningful. Trust begins to grow. We stop trying to impose solutions and instead create space for authentic connection.

Intentionality in relationships doesn't just transform ministry—it transforms the science of human relationships. Studies in psychology show that setting intentions for interactions strengthens relationships and fosters trust. Sacred Listening builds on this principle by grounding that intentionality in our faith, opening the door for a more profound connection.

Alignment: Listening in a Way That Resonates

But the theologically informed intention is only one component. The second key aspect of Sacred Listening is alignment, which comes from communication theory. This is about listening in a way that aligns with the needs and preferences of the person you're with. It's not enough to just hear someone. You need to listen in a way that makes them *feel* heard. This might mean different things for different people.

Young people today communicate in a variety of ways—through texts, social media, art, and even silence. If we insist on communicating in ways that feel comfortable for us but alien to them, we miss the point. Sacred Listening asks us to align our listening style with the person in front of us. For some, it's about maintaining eye contact and giving feedback in real time. For others, it's about following up on a text conversation days later. The key is to meet people where they are, not where we wish they would be. This approach requires a great deal of empathy and humility.

While it might be difficult, research in communication supports this approach. When people feel that their preferred communication style is being respected, they're more likely to feel understood and valued. Sacred Listening is building trust and deepening relationships by listening in a way that truly resonates with the other person.

Pattern Recognition: Seeing the Larger Picture

Once we've set our intention and aligned our listening, Sacred Listening calls us to do something else: pay attention to the patterns. This element comes from sociology, the study of human behavior and social interactions. Sociology teaches us that while each person is unique, their experiences often reflect broader trends within their community or generation.

Sacred Listening encourages us to look for these patterns, not as a way to stereotype or generalize but as a tool for understanding. For example, if a student mentions feeling overwhelmed every Tuesday, that might seem like a small detail. But what if you hear the same thing from several other students? Is there something about their schedule or school environment that makes Tuesdays particularly tough? Or if you notice that a group of young people is feeling disconnected, is there a broader trend of loneliness or isolation in your community?

Social sciences give us tools to make sense of these patterns. By tracking what we hear and paying attention to recurring themes, we can begin to see where individual needs overlap with larger trends. Recognizing these patterns allows us to respond to deeper issues in our community while still honoring each person's unique story.

Sacred Listening also asks us to document these patterns. Writing things down might feel awkward or clinical at first, but it's actually a way of honoring the people we're listening to. Research in relational care suggests that documenting interactions improves follow-up and strengthens relationships. In ministry, keeping track of what people share ensures that no one slips through the cracks and that every voice is remembered.

Formative and Summative: Fummative?

Sacred Listening is designed to do more than just extract information from young people. Often, when we listen—whether in person or through surveys or data collection—the goal is to gather insights that help us shape our ministries. This summative approach serves its purpose by informing our next steps, but it only scratches the surface of what listening can achieve. Sacred Listening moves beyond this, recognizing that the process of listening itself can be formative. When done with care, listening builds trust, creates space for divine encounters, and strengthens relationships in ways that go far beyond simple data collection.

At the heart of Sacred Listening is the belief that young people need to experience being heard—not just for the information they provide but because their stories and voices matter. When we approach listening as an opportunity to build relationships, we allow young people to feel truly seen and valued. This shifts the focus from getting answers to fostering connection. The Sacred Listening tools at the ends of the chapters aren't just mechanisms to coax reluctant kids into sharing their thoughts—they are tools to nurture deeper bonds through genuine, attentive engagement.

When we listen in this way, the very act of listening becomes sacred. It isn't about trying to convert, evangelize, or steer young people in a particular direction in any particular interaction. It's about letting the conversation itself be enough. This approach takes direct inspiration from a quote most often attributed to the Mennonite theologian David Augsburger: "Being listened to is so close to being loved that most people cannot tell the difference." Sacred Listening allows us to build relationships not by gathering information to act on later but by being fully present in the moment, creating trust, and making space for something holy to happen between us and the young people we serve.

"Being listened to is so close to being loved that most people cannot tell the difference."

Sacred Listening in Action

The beauty of Sacred Listening is that it doesn't end with theory—it moves directly into practice. The Sacred Listening tools at the ends of the chapters are not separate steps but practical manifestations of how to put Sacred Listening into action. These tools are designed to guide you through the key elements of the theory—setting intentions, aligning with the person you're listening to, and recognizing patterns—while also helping you apply them in real-life ministry.

Each tool is built around the principles of Sacred Listening. They'll guide you in setting intentions, asking the right questions, and tracking the patterns that emerge from your conversations. But more importantly, they'll help you follow up in ways that show you care—not just in theory but in practice. Whether you're checking in with a student on a tough day or creating new spaces for connection, Sacred Listening tools give you the structure to make your ministry more relational, more effective, and more sacred.

These tools, developed by the extraordinary Megan Bissell, my cofounder at Future of Faith, have been developed from years of listening to young people.[4] Together, Megan and I have learned one very important lesson: Large, national datasets aren't that helpful for people trying to make a real impact in the lives of young people.

If you're a youth minister in Tallahassee, it's just not all that useful for you to know what's going on with young people in Seattle. But that's essentially what massive datasets from national studies offer you. Maybe they're interesting, but they're not very useful. We know. Together Megan and I built one of the largest datasets about religion and young people that has ever been produced.

No matter how much data we collect, we can never bridge the gap from information to action. Knowing that 30 percent of young people are lonely doesn't help you know what to do about Jeremy, the young person whom you're having coffee with later today. Jeremy isn't one-third lonely or lonely one-third of the time. And it's probably not even true that one-third of the young people you interact with are lonely, because lonely young people are not evenly distributed. So while that information might be useful for a policymaker, national nonprofit, or denominational leader, it doesn't really do you much good. And this book is for you, not them, and what you need is not information about young people in general. You need information about the young people sitting across from you, the young people in your community.

At the same time, you cannot treat young people like research subjects in a lab or animals on display, collecting data without real connection. The young people in your community are not anonymous survey respondents—they are people you know. That is why the tools at the ends of the chapters prioritize a human-centered approach to research.

We recognize that every interaction is an opportunity for ministry, so we've built tools that will help you do two things simultaneously. First and most importantly, they will help you connect directly with young people in intentional, meaningful ways that communicate your care and concern for them. In

---

4. The Sacred Listening tools provided at the end of chaps. 1–6 are abbreviated versions, mostly for illustration purposes. For full, step-by-step, free versions of these exercises, see www.futureoffaith.org/sacredlisteningtools.

this way, you'll have expanded opportunities for ministry and interaction with young people around the issues that are most pressing to them.

To truly reach young people in a relational way, you need to track some key aspects of their lives so you can scale relational ministries to the same level that we once scaled programs. So the second thing our tools will help you do is ask just the right questions to easily collect and input information that is actionable at a glance. For example, at the end of chapter 4 we describe a simple check-in tool that will allow anyone in your organization to know which young people are most disconnected in your community or are experiencing a rough season of life.

At the end of each exercise, we show you how to take your unique data and use it to scale your relational ministry beyond your own individual capacity. After all, we'll never be able to transition away from programs toward relationships if we're just relying on the number of contacts that one person can maintain.

We've spent our entire careers as researchers collecting data from people in all walks of life, and we firmly believe that listening to people's stories and experiences, whether in an interview, survey, focus group, or quick check-in, is sacred work.

We believe that if someone is willing to share something about their life with you, you owe it to them to take it seriously. Capture the information in some way. Write it down, put it on a spreadsheet, or send yourself a quick note. Honor the vulnerability and truth of that other person. And then do something about it.

Sacred Listening is not just an idea; it's a way of living out your ministry in every interaction. The tools are designed to ensure that the theory doesn't remain abstract but becomes a tangible process for building deeper relationships, fostering trust, and ultimately transforming lives.

What we aim to do with the tools in this book is simply to offer some structured ways that have been proven to help make that endeavor easier and more accessible for everyone. Even though the tools are grounded in solid academic research, they do not require any research experience or specialization to be used effectively. All you need to do is care. And we know you have that part locked in already. We're just here to help your caring go further.

Scaling Relationships: Up, Out, and Down

Implicit in the idea of Sacred Listening is that we must rethink what we mean by "scale" in ministry. As conventional religious participation declines, the challenge for ministries is not just to build more connections but to build deeper and more transformative ones. This goes beyond the traditional notion of "scaling up," where success is measured by growing numbers. Instead, ministries today must scale in three dimensions—up, out, and down—to ensure that their impact is both wide reaching and personally meaningful.

"Scaling up" refers to expanding the impact of ministry, not by increasing staff or resources but by making smarter, more strategic use of what is already available. Sacred Listening tools make this possible by enabling ministries to collect and use relational insights in a systematic way. Rather than simply expanding numbers, these tools help ministries grow by enabling them to customize their messages and interactions to meet the real needs of large audiences. The data collected through Sacred Listening doesn't just inform; it transforms how ministries understand and engage with their communities, making large-scale impact possible even with limited resources.

"Scaling out" involves broadening the scope of ministry by empowering more people to engage in relational work. Sacred Listening tools help track critical information that enables community members—volunteers, lay leaders, and others—to step into relational roles with confidence. These tools don't just identify who needs attention but also give the community the insights they need to have the right conversations at the right time. By decentralizing ministry and encouraging greater participation, Sacred Listening fosters a culture of shared responsibility, ensuring that no one is left behind and that ministry extends into new communities and demographics.

Finally, "scaling down" is perhaps the most transformative dimension. It's about going deeper into relationships more quickly and effectively. Sacred Listening tools are designed around the recognition that we simply do not get as much time with young people as we once did. They are simply not as engaged with our religious institutions as they were in the past, when youth ministers could count on developing a relationship with a young person and their family slowly, over time. In short, we need to go deeper faster.

Sacred Listening tools are built to allow ministries to scale in a way that makes relationships—not just numbers—the measure of success. Scaling up extends reach, scaling out increases engagement, and scaling down deepens relationships. This approach redefines what it means to "scale" in ministry, ensuring that growth is not just expansive but also transformative.

A Note About Theology

I'm a sociologist, not a theologian. Unlike in a lot of youth ministry books you might read, you won't find any theology in this one. I promise. I will stay in my lane. I don't think any of you need me to provide theological justification for why you should connect with young people. I'm thoroughly convinced that you all will do that far better than I ever could.

However, while I'm a sociologist of religion, I'm also a religious sociologist. I grew up in a religious household and have worked and worshiped in a variety of religious settings throughout my life. I believe my work as a sociologist is a calling. We are all created in the image of God, and as I mentioned above, the act of getting to listen to someone's story is essentially a sacred act. I believe it is an encounter with the divine. So while you won't find Scripture or explicit theology in the following pages, you will find a healthy dose of that perspective.

The exercises and insights in this book are grounded in science, data, and good methodology, but they've been selected and adapted for presentation here because I fundamentally believe that when we stop to listen to one another and take time to truly understand one another, God is revealed and both parties are better off. In this case, young people will be changed through the revelation of an adult who cares enough to pay deep attention, and you'll be changed by seeing God constantly in the experiences, thoughts, and life of the young person.

At least, that's what I've experienced. I hope and pray the same is true for you.

Looking Ahead

New generations often require a shift in approach to ministry. Sometimes, those shifts are small and subtle. We begin emailing or texting invitations to come to youth group instead of sending out mailers or making phone calls.

And sometimes, a change in the culture requires a much more dramatic shift. The loss of institutional trust, for example, means that we need to fundamentally rethink how we and our organizations position ourselves in the lives of young people.

But one thing is clear: Change is inevitable. The famous data scientist W. Edwards Deming is said to have remarked, "It is not necessary to change. Survival is not required." That sentiment very much captures where the church is right now.

We are at a moment in time when the survival of our religious traditions is very much in question. I will cover some of that data in the coming chapters, but I'm guessing you probably already know much of it. It's alarming. Attendance, belief, and affiliation rates have all been declining for decades.[5] We simply cannot afford to continue doing things the way we have always done. We also should not fool ourselves into thinking that small tweaks to the system are going to be enough. One way or another, the future is going to be very different.

---

5. "In U.S., Decline of Christianity Continues at Rapid Pace: An Update on America's Changing Religious Landscape," Pew Research Center, October 17, 2019, https://www.pewresearch.org/religion/2019/10/17/in-u-s-decline-of-christianity-continues-at-rapid-pace/.

With all that in mind, many of the topics outlined in the chapters of this book will require you to rethink the way you're connecting with young people today. I won't ask you to make changes blindly. There's good science and practical exercises to help you make changes where you see that they are needed. Use what you need or find helpful; disregard the rest.

"It is not necessary to change. Survival is not required."

What we need to clarify before moving any further, though, is exactly what kinds of changes are necessary. Nobody should be entertaining a change to their beliefs, values, or ideology. Even young people aren't asking you to do that. In fact, they would see any changes to core beliefs as inauthentic.

But we can change the way we communicate our beliefs and engage with the next generations. When I was a kid, youth group lock-ins filled with pizza and caffeine were all the rage. They were wildly effective for me and my friends to see church as a place where we belonged. But it's not decreed in the New Testament that you have to host a lock-in for all the middle schoolers in your community at least once a year. The way we connect with young people can and should change to match their reality.

My goal in writing this book is for you to gain both a new understanding of the fundamental dynamics influencing emerging generations today and a couple new tools in your tool kit to help you do what you do best: care for young people.

Before we get into the chapters, I just want to say thank you. Thank you for all that you do to care for young people. I know sometimes the work can feel daunting and lonely and like you aren't making as much progress as you'd like. But as someone who has helped to collect tens of thousands of data points from young people and, more importantly, as someone who is the father of a fourteen-year-old, I can tell you that a caring adult makes all the difference in the life of a young person today. Indeed, it's the only thing that ever has. So thank you, from the bottom of my heart, for all that you do for young people to bring them closer to God.

GEN Z AND GEN ALPHA

What Is a Generation?

The way we've been thinking about generations doesn't work anymore. Traditionally, we've taken a one-size-fits-all approach to explaining what makes up the unique attributes of a group of people who happen to have been born between two otherwise random dates on the calendar. It's convenient shorthand to refer to generations, but it can lead to some real problems as well. As Pew Research Center noted recently, generational classifications have several specific problems:

1. Generational categories are not defined or agreed on by scientists or academics.
2. Like all labels, generational labeling often results in stereotyping, obscuring important points of diversity.
3. Traditional notions of generational classification focus on differences, often for the purposes of marketing or headlines.
4. There is an upper-class bias in the way we typically think about generations.

5. People are not static. Individuals and even whole groups change.[1]

Pew is right about all this, of course. But I think we should add to their list one more very important thing: Thinking about generations in the traditional way isn't very useful. That really should be the guiding star for religious leaders and people working in ministry. What will help us connect with young people in the most effective way? Traditional thinking about generational categories simply isn't part of that answer. I've always said that as a researcher, author, and scholar I want to be *useful*, not just interesting. I'm guessing that's how you feel about your work too.

In this chapter, I'll examine where our focus should be as we think about young people to help avoid falling into the trap of traditional generational thinking. However, to make it clear whom I'm talking about, I'll still often refer to young people by their generational categories. What you'll notice, though, is that I won't make broad claims about those generations or offer overly simplistic, bullet-point lists about what characterizes them relative to other age cohorts. Instead, I'll be trying to shift the focus to the social and cultural dynamics and experiences that shape young people today.

Who Is a Generation?

First, let's offer some conceptual clarity about whom exactly we're referring to when we talk about Gen Z and Gen Alpha. Social scientists largely, though not uniformly, consider Gen Z to be anyone born between 1997 and 2013 and Gen Alpha to be those young people born after 2013.[2] Effectively, this means that in 2024,

---

1. Michael Dimock, "5 Things to Keep in Mind When You Hear About Gen Z, Millennials, Boomers and Other Generations," Pew Research Center, May 22, 2023, https://www.pewresearch.org/short-reads/2023/05/22/5-things-to-keep-in-mind-when-you-hear-about-gen-z-millennials-boomers-and-other-generations/.

2. "What Is Generation Alpha?," *Casey Connects* (blog), Annie E. Casey Foundation, updated January 19, 2024, https://www.aecf.org/blog/what-is-generation

Gen Z includes people who are eleven to twenty-seven years old and Gen Alpha is anyone under age eleven.

Of course, these are not hard and fast boundaries. Use them as general categories of understanding and take them with a big grain of salt. Anyone who has ever been caught in a discussion where someone was going on about how they're a "geriatric millennial" understands just how pointless it is to try and nail down generations with razor-like precision. Interesting? Maybe. Useful? Not really.

It's more useful to think about what shaped someone's coming-of-age years, similar to the approach Jean Twenge takes in her recent book, *Generations: The Real Differences Between Gen Z, Millennials, Gen X, Boomers, and Silents and What They Mean for America's Future*. What life events have permeated their general consciousness, if not determined their collective behavior? Gen Zers will have lived through COVID, Trump, and the explosion of social media during their formative years. Gen Alpha, while still young, will be the first generation to grow up in a world increasingly characterized by artificial intelligence, a United States where Christians and people who identify as white are the plurality but not the majority, and an incredibly polarized political environment.[3]

It's helpful to have these basic distinctions down as we move forward in this book, but again, these distinctions are not as critical as people like to think. Thinking about generations in the traditional way, where we make claims that "millennials are _____" or "baby boomers value _____," increasingly leads to a lot of misunderstanding and, ultimately, miscalculation in terms of how we engage with young people. In a world as diverse as the one we live in now, this kind of thinking leads to a lot of stereotypes that not only are untrue but make it harder for us to be effective in how

---

-alpha; Michael Dimock, "Defining Generations: Where Millennials End and Generation Z Begins," Pew Research Center, January 17, 2019, https://www.pewresearch.org/fact-tank/2019/01/17/where-millennials-end-and-generation-z-begins/.

3. "Modeling the Future of Religion in America," Pew Research Center, September 13, 2022, https://www.pewresearch.org/religion/2022/09/13/modeling-the-future-of-religion-in-america/.

we build relationships with these groups. A mental model in which we make broad claims about a diverse group of people inherently leaves so many out that it harms more than it helps.

Kids These Days

But this is nothing new. Sometimes when I give talks about generations, I like to start with a small quiz. Here it is: You get a point if you can guess who said each of the following quotes or the year of the quote. Actually, you get a point if you can even guess the right century (see footnotes for correct answers).

> "They think they know everything, and are always quite sure about it."[4]
>
> "The young people of today think of nothing but themselves. They have no reverence for parents or old age. They are impatient of all restraint. They talk as if they alone knew everything and what passes for wisdom with us is foolishness with them."[5]
>
> "The free access which many young people have to romances, novels, and plays has poisoned the mind and corrupted the morals of many a promising youth."[6]
>
> "We defy anyone who goes about with his eyes open to deny that there is, as never before, an attitude on the part of young folk which is best described as grossly thoughtless, rude, and utterly selfish."[7]

---

4. Aristotle, *Rhetoric* 2.12, fourth century BCE. *Rhetoric by Aristotle*, trans. W. Rhys Roberts (Mockingbird Classics, 2015).

5. Peter the Hermit, thirteenth century CE. This quote is commonly attributed to a sermon by Peter the Hermit, but the original source has not been found. See, e.g., Tanya Byron, "'We See Children as Pestilent,'" *Guardian*, March 16, 2009, https://www.theguardian.com/education/2009/mar/17/ephebiphobia-young-people-mosquito.

6. Reverend Enos Hitchcock, eighteenth century. *Memoirs of the Bloomsgrove Family* [. . .] (Boston, 1790), 189.

7. Editorial in *Hull Daily Mail*, twentieth century. Amanda Ruggeri, "People Have Always Whinged About Young Adults. Here's Proof," *BBC*, October 3, 2017,

"[Young people have forced us to] become accustomed to preeners and posers who don't have anything to offer except themselves and their need to be on the public stage."[8]

Adults have been complaining about teenagers for as long as there have been teenagers. It's sort of an immutable truth. So just keep in mind, before you make sweeping claims about "kids these days," maybe what you really mean is just "kids." In other words, maybe kids have always been this way, and it's not about a particular generation at all.

My favorite way of summing all this up is from Elspeth Reeve. In an article for *The Atlantic* in 2013, she counters the claim that all millennials, the generation born from 1981 to 1996, are narcissistic. Elspeth writes, "Basically, it's not that people born after 1980 are narcissists, it's that young people are narcissists, and they get over themselves as they get older. It's like doing a study of toddlers and declaring those born since 2010 are *Generation Sociopath: Kids These Days Will Pull Your Hair, Pee On Walls, Throw Full Bowls of Cereal Without Even Thinking of the Consequences.*"[9]

We Are Almost Certainly Mistaken

These sentiments about generations are more than simply amusing. The way we think about groups of people is affected by a host of social and psychological phenomena that have a real impact on the way we believe and behave. For example, in 2023 two researchers from Columbia University and Harvard University teamed up to analyze over twelve million survey responses across sixty nations

---

https://www.bbc.com/worklife/article/20171003-proof-that-people-have-always-complained-about-young-adults.

8. Peter Kluger, twenty-first century. Brooke Lea Foster, "The Persistent Myth of the Narcissistic Millennial," *Atlantic*, November 19, 2014, https://www.theatlantic.com/health/archive/2014/11/the-persistent-myth-of-the-narcissistic-millennial/382565/.

9. Elspeth Reeve, "Every Every Every Generation Has Been the Me Me Me Generation," *Atlantic*, May 9, 2013, https://www.theatlantic.com/national/archive/2013/05/me-generation-time/315151/ (emphasis original).

and seventy years to study moral decline.[10] They found that people in every country and generation robustly agree that morality is on the decline. Over and over again they were able to show that respondents perceived that the world was less moral than it used to be and that respondents had felt this way for decades and perhaps longer (the data only go back so far).

Would you agree? Does the world seem like it's lost its way? That people don't treat each other with civility and respect anymore? I actually hear this quite a lot in Q&As. Someone will ask me not *if* morality has declined but rather what we should do as leaders *given that* morality has declined so much with this generation.

However, as the researchers have concluded, it is almost certainly not the case that morality is on the decline. The following is a summary of their findings:

> Participants in the foregoing studies believed that morality has declined, and they believed this in every decade in every nation we studied. They believed the decline began somewhere around the time they were born, regardless of when that was, and they believed it continues to this day. They believed the decline was a result both of individuals becoming less moral as they move through time and of the replacement of more moral people by less moral people. And they believed that the people they personally know and the people who lived before they did are exceptions to this rule. *About all of these things, they were almost certainly mistaken.*[11]

The conclusion that people are "almost certainly mistaken" about actual moral decline rests on a couple things. First, if morality were actually decreasing in each successive generation, and by the amounts that people recorded, the world would be unsafe and disorderly. And yet, that is not the case. Second, despite their concerns about overall morality, people are not reporting that they are being treated any differently.

10. Adam M. Mastroianni and Daniel T. Gilbert, "The Illusion of Moral Decline," *Nature* 618 (2023): 782–89.
11. Mastroianni and Gilbert, "Illusion of Moral Decline," 787–88 (emphasis added).

So how can it be true that people everywhere believe that each new generation of young people is less moral and driving society to collapse if the objective evidence doesn't line up? The researchers point to negativity bias as a key part of the answer.

Negativity Bias

Negativity bias is a well-known cognitive bias that explains our tendency to hold on to negative events more than positive ones. In other words, negative impressions tend to resonate and stick with us more than good impressions do. Aside from explaining why news headlines are so grim, this also helps us understand why so many adults think of young people in negative terms. The negative things that young people do stick with us.

But beyond our own bias is another very important piece of the puzzle. In the passage above, the researchers note that participants "believed that the people they personally know" are the exceptions. People conclude that while the world is less moral, they and their friends are not; they are just as moral as ever. As mind-boggling as this is, it is not uncommon.

As human beings, we are inclined to think of people in our inner circle differently than we think of strangers. We are more forgiving, slower to judge, and less likely to stereotype those in our inner circle. But we paint with broad strokes and make overly generalized claims about those on the outside. While we might explain an error by a close friend as a simple mistake or lapse in judgment, we are much more likely to explain the same transgression by someone outside our group as an attribute of "those people." Sociologists have described this phenomenon for years as basic in-group/out-group theory and have identified it as the root of a lot of the stereotypes and prejudices we hold.

You can see that same dynamic above in Mastroianni and Gilbert's research. The respondents in the study essentially conform to in-group bias. When applied to how adults think about young people, the implications are pretty clear. Unless we're very intentional about counteracting these natural cognitive and social biases, we're likely to focus on the negative, amplify it, and hold generations other than our own collectively accountable for it.

It's absolutely critical that we have a good framework for understanding young people and new generations accurately. Otherwise, we are subject to powerful social and psychological forces that do not always serve us or others well. If we think, for example, that newer generations are less moral than we were and are, then we will behave differently than if we simply assume that young people today are more or less the same as we were but operating in a vastly altered environment.

The assumption of a lack of morality could compel us to correct young people, chastise them for errors, and try to reeducate them so they can be as moral as we are. However, if we instead assess that young people are coming of age in a context very different from the one we grew up in but make decisions in more or less the same way, then we can meet them in those moments and help them work out the consequences of any particular decision with grace, love, and forgiveness.

These are enormously different approaches. I think we've seen the lack of usefulness in the correctional approach, and it's pretty clear to me that we need a new pathway forward that doesn't rely on thinking about generations as distinct containers with predictable, broken behaviors on the basis of a simple range of birth dates. We need to start paying better attention to the factors at work in the world.

Bias Containers

We need to change the way we think about generations for two primary reasons. First, we have reached a point in our society where the diversity of each successive generation is so great that any attempt at defining a generation with a singular word, phrase, or even list of characteristics is unlikely to apply to very many of them. Second, trying to categorize people is not a very effective way to understand them or to craft engagement strategies that will work.

Our newest generations are more diverse than we have ever experienced in every possible way. In fact, you could argue that Gen Z and Gen Alpha are the most diverse generations that have ever existed anywhere in the world at any given time. This makes characterizing these generations with an adjective or set of adjectives incredibly difficult and likely inaccurate.

The truth is that generations have never been as monolithic as we like to think. In this way, generational thinking is often simply a container for bias. There's always been more diversity than is accounted for in most of the overly broad characterizations of generations.

For instance, what people mostly mean when they talk about "baby boomers" or "Gen X" or some other generation are the upper-middle-class, suburban, predominantly white members of that generation.[12] Perhaps fifty years ago this would have captured enough of the cohort that our characterizations could still have had some predictive power. But if you're a ministry, business, nonprofit, or any other organization today trying to reach young people, an understanding rooted in upper-middle-class, suburban, predominantly white members of that group really will not capture many of them at all.

The diversity of Gen Z and Gen Alpha is reflected in their demographics, attitudes, and beliefs. Let's look at just a handful of statistics to really understand the unprecedented levels of diversity among young people today.

Race and Ethnicity

Gen Z is the most racially and ethnically diverse generation in the United States, with nearly half identifying as non-white. Similarly, Gen Alpha is projected to be the first majority-minority generation in the US, with over half its population expected to be non-white by 2060. According to the Pew Research Center, 48 percent of Gen Zers are non-white, compared to 39 percent of

---

12. William Strauss and Neil Howe, *Generations: The History of America's Future, 1584 to 2069* (Quill William Morrow, 1991).

millennials, 30 percent of Gen Xers, 21 percent of baby boomers, and 15 percent of the Silent Generation. Gen Alpha is even more diverse than Gen Z.[13] In 2022 just under half of all children were white (49 percent), and by 2050 the projections tell us that 61 percent of all children will be non-white.[14]

Gen Zers are more likely to have friends of different races and ethnicities than previous generations. According to Pew, 68 percent of Gen Zers say that some of their best friends are a different race or ethnicity from themselves, compared to 59 percent of millennials, 49 percent of Gen Xers, and 40 percent of baby boomers.[15]

Immigration

Gen Zers are also more likely to be children of immigrants. In the US, 22 percent of Gen Zers have at least one foreign-born parent, compared to 14 percent of millennials, 11 percent of Gen Xers, and 7 percent of baby boomers.[16]

Religion

Gen Z is less likely to identify as Christian and more likely to be religiously unaffiliated than previous generations. According to Pew, 26 percent of Gen Zers are religiously unaffiliated, compared to 21 percent of millennials, 16 percent of Gen Xers, and 11 percent of baby boomers.[17]

---

13. *Understanding Generation Alpha: The Most Diverse Generation Yet* (Hotwire Global, 2019), https://www.hotwireglobal.com/whitepaper/generation-alpha-2/.

14. Office of the Chief Statistician, *America's Children: Special Issue 2024, Maternal and Infant Health and Well-Being*, US Office of Management and Budget, ChildStats, https://www.childstats.gov/americaschildren/.

15. US Census Bureau, "2020 Census Reveals the Changing Face of America," August 2021, https://www.census.gov/library/stories/2021/08/2020-census-reveals-the-changing-face-of-america.html.

16. "8 Facts About Generations and How They Vote," Pew Research Center, November 14, 2019, https://www.pewresearch.org/fact-tank/2019/11/14/8-facts-about-generations-and-how-they-vote/.

17. "In U.S., Decline of Christianity Continues at Rapid Pace: An Update on America's Changing Religious Landscape," Pew Research Center, October 17, 2019, https://www.pewresearch.org/religion/2019/10/17/in-u-s-decline-of-christianity-continues-at-rapid-pace/.

Social Issues

Gen Z is more likely to support same-sex marriage than previous generations. According to the Public Religion Research Institute (PRRI), 70 percent of Gen Zers support same-sex marriage, compared to 53 percent of millennials, 44 percent of Gen Xers, and 38 percent of baby boomers.[18]

Gen Z is more likely to support gender equality than previous generations. According to the Pew Research Center, 70 percent of Gen Zers believe that women should have equal rights with men in all areas, compared to 65 percent of millennials, 61 percent of Gen Xers, and 56 percent of baby boomers.[19]

Household Arrangement

Gen Z is more likely to have grown up in a household with two working parents than previous generations. According to Pew, 61 percent of Gen Zers grew up in a household with two working parents, compared to 57 percent of millennials, 50 percent of Gen Xers, and 46 percent of baby boomers.[20]

Coming to grips with a world that is too diverse to lend itself to thinking about generations as one-size-fits-all containers has a tremendous impact on our ministries. Our work with young people must be much less homogeneous and instead geared to work with, not against, the realities present in their lives.

Hidden Diversity

It can be difficult to come to terms with the diversity present in the lives of young people, because for many adults, it simply isn't

---

18. "Fractured Nation: Widening Partisan Polarization and Key Issues in 2020 Presidential Elections," PRRI, October 20, 2019, https://www.prri.org/research/fractured-nation-widening-partisan-polarization-and-key-issues-in-2020-presidential-elections/.

19. Kim Parker and Ruth Igielnik, "On the Cusp of Adulthood and Facing an Uncertain Future: What We Know About Gen Z So Far," Pew Research Center, May 14, 2020, https://www.pewsocialtrends.org/essay/on-the-cusp-of-adulthood-and-facing-an-uncertain-future-what-we-know-about-gen-z-so-far/.

20. Parker and Igielnik, "Cusp of Adulthood."

present in their own lives, even when they live with teenagers. It would actually be easy for many of us to miss the diversity present in this country because it's not evenly distributed. Our churches and neighborhoods are remarkably homogeneous. Seventy years after *Brown v. Board of Education* our schools are, by many statistical measures, more segregated than they were in 1953.[21] Even the way many adults use social media platforms creates a deepening of an echo chamber filled with people who look, talk, and act just like they do.

But this is not the case for young people. Youth culture has always been more diverse than the rest of society, and social media has greatly accelerated this dynamic. As we'll explore more in chapter 6, young people use social media platforms in remarkably different ways than adults. One of the clear differences is in the amount of diversity they encounter in these spaces and how this diversity is presented and celebrated.

Social psychologists recognize a variety of different social arrangements and groups, including primary groups and reference groups. Primary groups are the people close to you whom you look to for support, friendship, love, and so on. Think about your family and close friends. Maybe even some coworkers. Your reference group, on the other hand, is the group of people you look to as the standard for what or who you'd like to become. Reference groups provide a standard of behavior for living out values and identities but not the same kind of accountability that primary groups provide.

As we age, our primary groups and reference groups tend to converge. In other words, we end up becoming friends with people who are more or less like us. We've largely made the major decisions in our lives concerning values and identities that external reference groups are so helpful with.

---

21. Gary Orfield, Erica Frankenberg, Jongyeon Ee, and Jennifer B. Ayscue, "Harming Our Common Future: America's Segregated Schools 65 Years After Brown," The Civil Rights Project, UCLA, May 10, 2019, https://www.civilrightsproject.ucla.edu/research/k-12-education/integration-and-diversity/harming-our-common-future-americas-segregated-schools-65-years-after-brown.

Young people, on the other hand, are often much more driven by their reference groups as they explore identities, values, and a sense of self. This has always been the case. The difference for today's younger generations, though, is that their reference groups can be engaged with, explored, created, and defined in real time through social media.

And these reference groups are incredibly diverse. The people they care about, respect, listen to, and are guided by are diverse not only in their identities but also in the value they have for diversity generally. The communities young people aspire to are not at all homogeneous, even if their in-person communities often are.

There are clear implications for ministries in all this. To engage generations who turn to diverse people and groups as the standard-bearers in their lives, we can't show up as a single source claiming to have all the answers without doing some serious listening first.

The convergence of primary and reference groups as one ages reflects a settling into established networks that affirm and reflect one's own values and identities. This gradual shift to homogeneity in personal associations often aligns with a period in life where individuals are less inclined to make drastic changes in their belief systems or social circles. Ministries have traditionally capitalized on this stability, offering programs and services that cater to this desire for affirmation within a community of like-minded individuals. However, the challenge and opportunity now lie in addressing the fluid and evolving nature of younger generations' social constructs.

For ministries, recognizing the dynamic and formative role of social media in shaping the identities of young people is crucial. Platforms such as Instagram, TikTok, and X (formerly Twitter) are not merely distractions or entertainment; they are virtual workshops where young individuals craft and test their identities. Ministries must understand that for Generations Z and Alpha, online interactions are as significant as face-to-face encounters, if not more so. Therefore, creating a digital presence is not about transplanting traditional messages onto new platforms but about fostering an authentic engagement that resonates with the interactive and participatory culture of these platforms.

Moreover, ministries must acknowledge the high value placed on diversity by these younger cohorts. They need to move beyond mere tolerance or inclusion of different viewpoints and backgrounds to celebrating and actively engaging with diversity. This means creating spaces—both online and offline—where difficult conversations about faith, values, and social issues can occur without judgment or presupposition. It's about the ministry acting as a facilitator for dialogue rather than a didactic authority. By doing so, ministries can become a part of the broader discourse that shapes young lives, rather than an echo chamber that fails to reach them.

Such an approach requires deep listening and a genuine openness to change. It may involve rethinking organizational structures, leadership styles, and communication strategies. Leaders within these ministries need to be as diverse as the communities they seek to serve. This diversity isn't just ethnic or racial; it encompasses a breadth of life experiences, thought processes, and theological perspectives. Training for ministry leaders should include not only traditional doctrine but also contemporary social issues, cultural competency, and digital communication expertise. The goal is for the ministry to reflect the multifaceted, interconnected world in which Generations Z and Alpha live.

In practice, this translates to ministries not only providing services and guidance but also learning from the individuals they serve. It involves inviting young people to lead and shape the programs that will serve them, ensuring these initiatives are relevant and responsive to their needs. By doing so, ministries can become allies in the search for meaning and community, which defines the journey of these emerging generations. They can cultivate a space where faith and identity are explored in concert with the reality of a changing world—a world where diversity of thought and experience are not only acknowledged but empowered.

Was I a Good Student?

As mentioned above, the second major reason why we need to change the way we think of generations has to do with utility. Even if we *could* find a way to characterize the youngest generations according to a few criteria or descriptors, the fact is that thinking about people in terms of the categories they fit into is actually not all that helpful in how we connect with them around life's biggest questions. As noted above, it may be interesting, but not all that useful. This is true for a number of reasons, but primarily because people do not behave in uniformly consistent ways, which makes our attempt to categorize and then predict their behavior on the basis of those categories unreliable at best.

One of my favorite sociologists, Howard Becker, makes this same point while arguing that we should focus on types of activities rather than types of people.[22] People, he notes, behave differently depending on the situation they're in, which makes categories not all that helpful for providing consistent insight into future behavior. To use a statistical term, categorical thinking has low predictive power.

Let me provide just one small example to help bring this to life. When I was a professor, I often asked my students if they thought I had been a good student when I was younger. The answer, nearly universally, was that I had indeed been a good student. They cited my going to graduate school, earning a PhD, and securing a job as a tenured faculty member as evidence. How could I *not* have been a good student?

I would then reveal that my high school grades were poor and hadn't earned me a single scholarship. My first two exam grades in my college physics course didn't add up to a passing grade. I sometimes chose not to study for exams and even turned in first drafts of papers as my final submission (which I'm sure still gives my English professors nightmares).

Did that change their assessment of me? Were these revelations enough to label me a bad student? Not at all. I was still seen as a good student; these were viewed as minor setbacks. What if I had failed a class or two? What if I had been expelled for poor

---

22. Howard S. Becker, *Tricks of the Trade: How to Think About Your Research While You're Doing It* (University of Chicago Press, 1998).

performance, only to come back and graduate at the top of my class? Where do we draw the line between a good student and a bad student?

You see the point. It's nearly impossible to draw boundaries like this. People's lives simply don't fit neatly into one category or label, especially when we start adding value judgments like "good" or "bad."

The same outcome occurred when I would ask my class to raise their hands if they thought of themselves as a good friend. I would ask them to put their hands down if they had ever lied to a friend or cheated them in some way. Every time I did this exercise I would watch all the hands in the room drop. Then, I would ask them to put them back up if they still thought of themselves as a good friend, and nearly every hand would go back up.

> If good students fail tests and good friends lie to each other, how are we to expect that everyone we shove into the box of Gen Z will behave in a predictable way?

Our common thinking about generations often falls into this same trap. We construct categories that are impossible to fit people into and do not have much predictive power at all. If good students fail tests and good friends lie to each other, how are we to expect that everyone we shove into the box of Gen Z will behave in a predictable way?

To Becker's point, categories become effectively useless—or actually damaging—because they lead us to think we can count on people to behave in a particular way that simply doesn't turn out to be true. The student who turns in sloppy work can't be counted on to always turn in sloppy work. The millennial who is behaving narcissistically as a teenager is not inherently self-centered. As Becker puts it, "Types that don't *actually* predict what they are supposed to aren't much use."[23]

---

23. Becker, *Tricks of the Trade*, 44 (emphasis added).

Situational Ministry

Becker suggests we should turn our focus to thinking about the situation itself instead of obsessing about categorizing people into groups with low predictability and impersonal judgments. Instead of asking if I was a good student, we should ask about the conditions that might get an otherwise good student to turn in sloppy work, even for a course in my major.

We will find out many more useful things if we consider the influences on someone's behavior instead of using that behavior to stamp them with positive or negative attributes. For example, we would learn that although I was an otherwise good student, I was lonely after a breakup with a romantic partner and started hanging around with new friends who didn't value academics, which led to a loss of focus and a shift in my priorities. Having this kind of insight would allow for a targeted solution rather than simply trying to figure out if I fit into the box of a "good" or "bad" student. It didn't mean that I was ready to quit school or that I needed a parent-teacher conference; I was just going through a hard time. You can probably imagine specific ways you could support postbreakup Josh already.

Perhaps more importantly, though, you would be able to communicate about similar experiences you had been through and even offer preemptive advice. You could be on the lookout for other students who are experiencing loneliness or sudden changes in social patterns and minister to them through the process. Your efforts would be focused not on trying to change yourself or others from one status to another (good to bad) but on helping deal with a particular set of conditions. Focusing on types of conditions allows you to design and implement solutions that are far more effective than trying to fundamentally change a person's core.

A minister's role is not to categorize but to comprehend and care. If we consider the gospel's core message of understanding and redemption, our approach to ministry must reflect a similar depth of empathy and action. Rather than reclassifying individuals on the basis of a perceived binary of moral- or performance-based categories, the ministry's real work lies in addressing the underlying issues that affect behavior. Doing so not only aids in the immediate betterment of the individual's situation but also builds a foundation for lasting transformation.

In practical ministry, this understanding translates into a more nuanced approach to pastoral care and community support. It requires creating programs and services that acknowledge and address the multifaceted reasons behind someone's struggles. For instance, a student ministry might offer counseling services that provide a space for students to discuss their academic pressures in the context of their personal lives. It could also mean providing a community group that focuses on how to maintain academic diligence amid life's ups and downs, thereby equipping students with the resilience and tools to navigate their studies during times of personal turmoil.

Moreover, when ministries focus on situational conditions, they align themselves with the biblical principle that each person is a complex individual with unique challenges and gifts. This not only enables a more compassionate and effective response to individual needs but also reflects the diversity and richness of human experience that the church is called to embrace. Ministries can thus become a reflection of the society they aim to serve, one that understands the interplay between personal challenges and societal expectations.

This approach also involves equipping leaders within the ministry to recognize and respond to signs of distress, isolation, or disengagement among their congregants or students. By training leaders to identify and address these issues proactively, ministries can prevent small challenges from becoming crises. Workshops, support groups, and one-on-one mentorship can all be parts of this preventive framework. Such proactive ministry does not wait for people to fall into "bad" categories; instead, it reaches out to guide them through their circumstances, offering redemptive support along the way.

Ultimately, this focus on conditions rather than categories redefines what a successful ministry looks like. Success is no longer about converting the bad into the good but about guiding everyone through whatever challenges they may face while affirming their worth and potential at every turn. It's about being Christlike shepherds who know their flock well enough to attend to each one according to their needs—a ministry not of judgment but of journeying together.

Enduring Trends

Rather than trying to reduce these generational members to a few characteristics that won't actually represent very many of them or falling into the trap of thinking that typical child development is somehow unique to this generation, we can look to two things that will help us more accurately understand what we're seeing from young people today: enduring trends and defining moments. Focusing on these two factors is important because they help shape the environment within which Gens Z and Alpha are making choices and decisions. It's a focus on processes as opposed to outcomes. Instead of saying, "Young people are _____," we should say, "The influences on young people today are _____."

The enduring social trends that are impacting young people today are all extensions of social and cultural dynamics that have been at work for decades, if not longer. We'll cover them in depth in the following chapters, but they are worth a quick examination here to help us shift our thinking from the old model of generational thinking toward something that more accurately reflects the realities young people face and is more informative for our own work with them.

The Trust Collapse

There has been no bigger influence on the social fabric of America than the loss of institutional trust we have experienced over the last fifty years. While this trend has been documented in numerous other countries around the world during the same time span, the loss is particularly profound for our country because so much of the character of the United States is founded on the idea that social institutions are rooted in the will, determination, and effort of the people.[24] Whether we're talking about government, religion, business, or social clubs, we have historically had high amounts of faith and confidence in our institutions.

Trust peaked in the years immediately following World War II, after the major institutions of our country came together to defeat the biggest evil known for generations, and it has been on the decline ever since. Social scientists might argue about *why* that trust has been lost, but nobody disputes the central premise. We simply do not have confidence in the basic building blocks of our society.

One of the effects of losing trust in institutions is that we've also lost faith in one another. In 2014, summing up the research on the decades-long decline of trust, researchers Jean Twenge, W. Keith Campbell, and Nathan Carter wrote, "Trust in others and confidence in institutions, two key indicators of social capital, reached historic lows among Americans in 2012 in two nationally representative surveys that have been administered since the 1970s."[25] And things have not improved since then. We are now in what Mark Malloch-Brown calls a "global trust recession,"[26] and as we'll see, there is plenty of data to back up that assertion.

Part of what makes this enduring social trend so strange, though, is that although the decline has been precipitous, you probably hardly have noticed it. It isn't something that occurred overnight. You likely didn't feel it from one year to the next, but the cumulative result of losing a little bit of trust every year for five decades is that we're living in a profoundly different society.

---

24. *2021 Edelman Trust Barometer*, Edelman, 2021, https://www.edelman.com/trust/2021-trust-barometer.

25. Jean M. Twenge, W. Keith Campbell, and Nathan T. Carter, "Declines in Trust in Others and Confidence in Institutions Among American Adults and Late Adolescents, 1972–2012," *Association for Psychological Science* 25, no. 10 (2014): 8.

26. Mark Malloch-Brown, "How to Rebuild Trust in Institutions: Results, Results, Results," World Economic Forum, December 18, 2023, https://www.weforum.org/agenda/2023/12/how-to-rebuild-trust-in-philanthropy-results-results-results/.

The impact on young people cannot be overstated. We now have a generation with little or no experience in trusting organizations of any kind because they're being raised by parents who don't trust organizations or the people who run them either. As we'll see in the next chapter, this gradual shift needs to be met with new strategies for engagement, and all too often the church is just behind the curve.

This Is the Church; This Is the Steeple . . .

Closely related to our loss of trust in institutions is the second enduring trend that is shaping young people: the changing nature of religious, spiritual, and faith expression. Religion was once primarily practiced in collective gatherings on Friday evenings or Sunday mornings and enjoyed widespread participation (if not actual adherence), but that is no longer the case. As Gallup reported in 2021, fewer than half of Americans are now members of a religious congregation.[27] This is the first time this has happened since social scientists began tracking these numbers.

Again, though, you can see that these numbers have not fallen off the table. Although the difference from the 1970s until today is a loss of nearly twenty-five points, it's been a gradual decline. The result is probably what you have experienced in your own life. It's not so much that massive amounts of churches have closed, leaving vacant buildings on every corner (though that is coming),[28] it's just that they all seem a little less full. The facade remains intact, but it's standing on an increasingly shaky foundation.

This decline exists for other markers of institutional religious health and vitality as well. The increasing number of Nones (those with no religious affiliation),[29] Dones (people who reject

---

27. Jeffrey M. Jones, "U.S. Church Membership Falls Below Majority for First Time," Gallup, March 29, 2021, https://news.gallup.com/poll/341963/church-membership-falls-below-majority-first-time.aspx.

28. Mark Elsdon, ed., *Gone for Good? Negotiating the Coming Wave of Church Property Transition* (Eerdmans, 2024).

29. Ryan P. Burge, *The Nones: Where They Came From, Who They Are, and Where They Are Going*, 2nd ed. (Fortress, 2023).

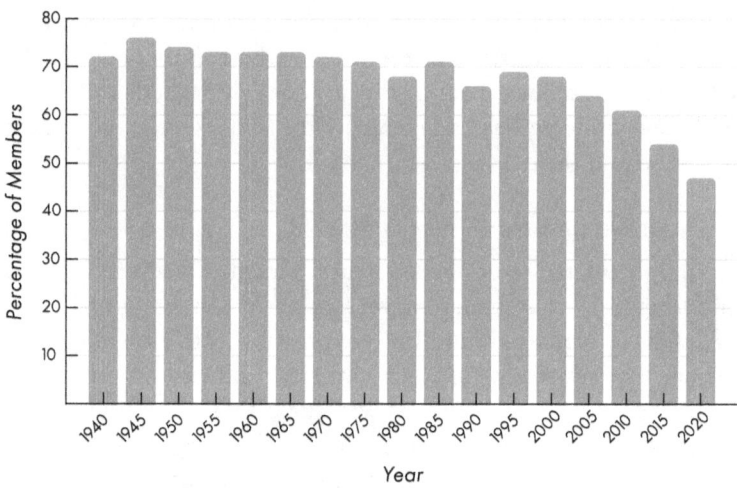

Church Membership Among US Adults (1940–2020)

institutional religious participation),[30] and "spiritual but not religious" groups has eroded the strength of formal institutional religion as a common touchstone experience for Americans.[31] Increasingly, young people are being raised in an environment where spiritual and religious exploration does not automatically mean that they attend a church, mosque, or synagogue. If my own students are any indicators, it's actually not uncommon for their only experiences with religious institutions to be weddings and funerals.

Scholars and others can and certainly do argue about the merits of shifting away from institutional practices of faith. But what is certain, regardless of how one feels about those institutions, is that it makes for a remarkably different kind of experience of the divine for young people. While our society is pretty well equipped to understand and support institutional expressions of faith, we

---

30. Josh Packard and Ashleigh Hope, *Church Refugees: Sociologists Reveal Why People Are Done with Church but Not Their Faith* (Group, 2015).

31. Jim Davis and Michael Graham, *The Great Dechurching: Who's Leaving, Why Are They Going, and What Will It Take to Bring Them Back?*, with Ryan P. Burge (Zondervan Reflective, 2023).

don't really know what to do with religious or spiritual needs outside that framework. We know how to offer prayer rooms, tax breaks, legal protections, and general social acceptance of institutional participation and identity, but we haven't built the same frameworks for faith practices, beliefs, and identities that fall outside those institutions.

The same is often true of ministries. Most know what to do with people when they show up, but many are at a loss otherwise. The pressing question for today's church leaders is how to engage with a generation that is less about rejecting faith and more about redefining it in noninstitutional terms. The task at hand is to facilitate a faith that resonates with individual search and collective experience, one that harnesses the communal power of the gospel to bridge the widening gap between traditional religion and contemporary spirituality. It is about creating a space where the spiritual journey is respected and supported in all its forms, ensuring that the church remains relevant and responsive in a rapidly changing world.

When young people grow up disconnected from traditional modes of religious expression, it can make for some pretty shaky territory. These young people often express that they don't really know how or if their religious and spiritual questions, beliefs, and expressions have a place in the modern world or who their guides should be. In chapter 3 I help explore how we can support them by shifting our tactics to reflect this new reality, but it's important here to understand that the environment that young people, and increasingly all Americans, are operating in is one where institutional participation as the default way of experiencing or expressing faith is on the decline and not likely to return any time soon.

The Doom Loop of Belonging

The final enduring trend influencing all young people concerns the human need to belong. Belonging, it turns out, is not just a desirable aspect of our lives; it is a fundamental need deeply ingrained in our biology and psychology. Researchers from diverse fields have uncovered fascinating insights into the importance of belonging in our lives.

Think back to Maslow's hierarchy of needs, which you probably learned about in a high school or college psychology class. Belongingness and love needs are right there, nestled in the core of our requirements. According to Maslow, our yearning for friendship, intimacy, and connection with others is not just a nice-to-have but a crucial component of our overall well-being and self-fulfillment.[32] It's one of the essential building blocks that sets the stage for our personal growth and flourishing. But it doesn't end there.

Numerous studies have unveiled the remarkable impact of social connection on our health outcomes.[33] It turns out that having strong social ties and support networks works wonders for our physical health. Those fortunate enough to enjoy robust connections tend to have reduced risks of chronic diseases, lower mortality rates, and quicker recovery from illnesses. It's as if our bodies thrive when we feel a sense of belonging and have a solid support system by our side.[34]

And the benefits extend beyond our physical welfare. Mental health and overall happiness are intricately tied to our social connections. Research consistently shows that people with a strong sense of belonging experience higher levels of well-being, lower rates of anxiety and depression, and greater resilience when faced with life's challenges. It's almost as if the warmth and support we receive from our social networks act as a shield, protecting our minds from the harsh blows of life.[35]

So it's no wonder that our social identities are deeply entwined with our sense of self. We find purpose, meaning, and shared

---

32. A. H. Maslow, "A Theory of Human Motivation," *Psychological Review* 50, no. 4 (1943): 370–96, https://doi.org/10.1037/h0054346.

33. Casper ter Kuile, *A Call to Connection: Rediscovering the Transformative Power of Relationships*, with Angie Thurston, Sue Phillips, and Derrick Scott III (Einhorn Collaborative, 2022).

34. Julianne Holt-Lunstad, Timothy B. Smith, and J. Bradley Layton, "Social Relationships and Mortality Risk: A Meta-Analytic Review," *PLOS Medicine* 7, no. 7 (2010), https://doi.org/10.1371/journal.pmed.1000316.

35. John T. Cacioppo and William Patrick, *Loneliness: Human Nature and the Need for Social Connection* (Norton, 2008).

values in our group affiliations. Being part of something larger than ourselves gives us a sense of identity and a place in the world.

But what happens when we find ourselves on the outskirts of belonging? That's where things take a dark turn. Social exclusion, the experience of being left out or disconnected, can have profound effects on our well-being. Neuroscientists have discovered that social exclusion triggers brain regions associated with emotional pain, revealing the deep emotional impact of feeling disconnected from others. It's as if our brains are hardwired to seek out belonging, and when it's absent, our very core feels the ache.[36]

Furthermore, belonging isn't just a modern-day luxury; it's deeply rooted in our evolutionary history. Throughout time, our survival has depended on our ability to form connections and foster communal bonds. Belonging to a group offered us cooperation, shared resources, and protection from threats. Our ancestors persevered because they had a sense of belonging encoded in their DNA.[37]

Belonging, it seems, is a vital human need. We are wired to connect, to belong. Yet Gen Z and Gen Alpha, the very generations that should be cultivating meaningful connections, forging lifelong bonds, and establishing their place in society, are grappling with a diminished sense of belonging.

Today, young individuals are facing dwindling opportunities to engage in community organizations and civic groups. The decline in youth membership rates across religious groups, sports teams, and volunteer organizations is indicative of a broader shift. It is as if we are caught in a doom loop of belonging. The opportunities for connection are waning, which means we have to work harder for even casual connections, which leads to people not

---

36. Naomi I. Eisenberger, Matthew D. Lieberman, and Kipling D. Williams, "Does Rejection Hurt? An fMRI Study of Social Exclusion," *Science* 302, no. 5643 (2003): 290–92, https://doi.org/10.1126/science.1089134.

37. Anjali Gireesan, "Evolution of Belongingness: Its Past, Present, and Future," in *Handbook of Health and Well-Being*, ed. Deb Sibnath and Brian A. Gerrard (Springer, 2022), https://doi.org/10.1007/978-981-16-8263-6_5.

seeking them as much as before. The result is that young people are adrift in a sea of isolation, unable and unwilling to meet even basic social needs.

Social media, once seen as a gateway to connection, often falls short of fostering genuine relationships. Shallow digital interactions cannot replace the warmth of face-to-face connections and the sense of belonging they provide. Moreover, the rise of cyberbullying and online exclusion has cast a dark shadow, leading to increased loneliness and anxiety and a diminished sense of belonging.

These challenges are taking a toll on the young mind; rising rates of anxiety and depression reflect young people's struggle to find their place in the world. By nearly every measure one can imagine, the mental health of today's young people is worse than at any time in history. Loneliness, anxiety, and depression were rising to record levels even before the pandemic.[38] At the root of much of this is a dwindling sense of belonging or being tied to a broader community of people who care about you, rely on you, celebrate you, and miss you when you're not there.

As we'll see in chapter 4, the decline in belonging has been underway for years. It is a social trend that, like the two above, will define today's youngest generations without direct intervention, but it didn't start with them. We're in the middle of a trend that has been at work for decades.

Defining Moments

Along with enduring trends are a couple of defining moments. I use the term "moments" here loosely, as the two moments that have affected Gen Z and Gen Alpha both stretch over a number of years: the global COVID-19 pandemic and the rise of social media.

38. Aubrianna Osorio, "Research Update: Children's Anxiety and Depression on the Rise," Georgetown University Center for Children and Families, March 24, 2022, https://ccf.georgetown.edu/2022/03/24/research-update-childrens-anxiety-and-depression-on-the-rise/.

COVID-19

The long-term impacts of the COVID-19 pandemic are still unfolding and touch nearly every aspect of physical, mental, spiritual, and social health. Young people who lived through school closures, quarantines, and disruptions to nearly all life's normal events are forever changed. However, we should not make the mistake of thinking that the impact of COVID was uniform.[39]

For example, there were massive disparities in health outcomes and unemployment that largely followed class breakdowns in the United States. Put simply, poor people were hit harder than others by the pandemic. Additionally, the virus proved much harder to recover from for older individuals and those who were immunocompromised. Aside from the very real human toll that the pandemic took on some groups and not others, we paid a social price as well.

Young people watched these disparities unfold while adults largely argued with one another over nearly every aspect of the pandemic response as the initial days of unity quickly gave way to fear, frustration, and competing human needs. One of the most helpful things I encountered to make sense of how the pandemic unfolded came from the disaster relief manual put out by the state of Nebraska.[40] In the manual, they reproduced a chart from two researchers documenting how disasters tend to unfold over time. Though the focus in the chart was on natural disasters, not pandemics and social disasters, you could see a lot of parallels.

As a country, sometimes it feels like we are still working our way through the disillusionment phase. Some of us are unsure if we will ever get to "reconstruction." Some days, it feels like we're there, but a lot of days it simply doesn't. If there is a social reconstruction to come, it will be young people leading the way.

39. Joseph Friedman, Mirza Balaj, Nazrul Islam et al., "Inequalities in COVID-19 Mortality: Defining a Global Research Agenda," *Bull World Health Organ* 100, no. 10 (2022): 648–50, https://doi.org/10.2471/BLT.22.288211.
40. "Phases of Disaster," Nebraska Strong Recovery Project, 2019, https://nebraskastrongrecoveryproject.nebraska.edu/wp-content/uploads/2020/08/Phases-of-Disaster-NE-Strong-English.pdf.

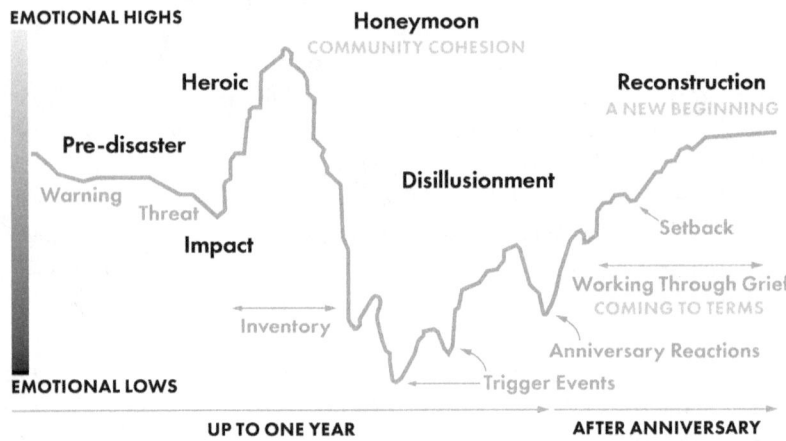

Source: Zunin/Meyers, as cited in Training Manual for Mental Health and Human Service Workers in Major Disasters, U.S. Department of Health and Human Services (2000).

It is critical as adults that we help young people process the impact of the pandemic in productive ways that lead to their individual and collective flourishing. Much of the pathway from disillusionment to reconstruction shown above involves working through grief, setbacks, and celebrations. Nobody is better situated than religious leaders to help young people put these moments in proper perspective. You have a host of intact rituals, sacred readings, and teachings that can help in this regard and a lifetime of knowledge and training to help craft new and meaningful ways of making sense of things that cannot be easily explained.

While the health consequences of the pandemic will diminish over time, the social and spiritual consequences will require ongoing intervention.

However, this moment must likely be met in new and creative ways if we are going to be of service to young people. If we're to assist young people in moving toward reconstruction, we're going to have to come to terms with the fact that many of the young people we come into contact with are dealing with things no teenager has ever had to deal with. We'll need to adjust our methods to meet the new realities of these generations.

As I suggest in chapter 5, it is absolutely critical for us to have a strong sense of what "business" we're in. The decades-long decline in trust and institutional participation was accelerated by the pandemic almost across the board. In particular, there appear to be ongoing and potentially permanent disruptions in three major areas that impact our ministry: the nature of faithfulness, adolescent mental health, and social skills.

(Anti-)Social Media

The second major defining moment concerns social media. Using the internet to directly connect with other people through apps and services like Discord (a messaging app similar to Slack or GroupMe), Instagram, Snapchat, X, Twitch, and others is still in its relative infancy, having started with Facebook less than two decades ago, but its impact has been monumental, especially for teenagers.

A myriad of studies have charted the growth of social media among young people, but if you take a look just at Pew's most recent report in this area, "Teens, Social Media and Technology 2022," you can get a sense of both the depth and the breadth of these apps among teenagers.[41] Over half of young people say it would be hard to give up social media at this point in their lives, nearly half say they use the internet "almost constantly," and over 15 percent of teenagers say they use YouTube, TikTok, and Snapchat "almost constantly." Additionally, they have seen how bad it can be for them. Over one-third of young people say they use social media too much.

As I write this, I'm seeing it unfold in my own house. My own teenage son, who is not allowed on social media, admitted to us that he needed help curtailing his screen time because he just couldn't

---

41. Emily A. Vogels, Risa Gelles-Watnick, and Navid Massarat, "Teens, Social Media and Technology 2022," Pew Research Center, August 10, 2022, https://www.pewresearch.org/internet/2022/08/10/teens-social-media-and-technology-2022/.

resist it. And in true young teenager fashion, when we stepped in to limit his screen time *at his request*, he got very, very angry.

But we hardly need statistics and studies to tell us what we know and see every day. You probably see it with your own kids and their friends. You probably see it with the kids you work with. Mobile social media has, in a very short amount of time, come to be an indispensable component of what it means to be a young person in America, for better or worse.

And there's a lot of evidence to suggest that, at least right now, it's for worse. In 2023, the US Surgeon General released an advisory calling attention to the urgent public health issues surrounding the harmful mental health consequences of social media use among teenagers.[42] The contents are concerning; they highlight the sensitive time of biological and social development that young teenagers are in at precisely the time they typically start engaging with social media. Although there are some positive effects of being able to communicate with people all around the world, there are negative consequences as well. With brains and biologies that are not fully developed, teenagers are in a battle trying to balance social media use and their own health.

As I found myself explaining to my son, this is not a fair fight. He is up against armies of PhDs who are employed and highly compensated to do nothing other than keep him glued to the screen. That is their entire job. The user experience is not engineered to maximize health or happiness; it's designed to make sure that you stay in the app for as long as possible and come back as often as possible. Of course our kids are having a hard time limiting their screen time. They don't stand a chance without our help.

Still, it's pretty clear that social media is not going away anytime soon. The 2022 Pew report cited above notes that over 95 percent of teenagers in the US have access to a smartphone, and over 90 percent of them have accessed social media. Never have we seen

---

42. Office of the Surgeon General, *Social Media and Youth Mental Health: The U.S. Surgeon General's Advisory*, US Department of Health and Human Services, last reviewed June 17, 2024, https://www.hhs.gov/sites/default/files/sg-youth-mental-health-social-media-advisory.pdf.

a new technology move so far and so quickly with young people. It's critical that we get a handle on how we're helping them navigate these online spaces so they can discover and live out their personal values and beliefs with integrity and emotional, mental, and social safety.

Conclusion

When you focus on these enduring trends and defining moments to help understand the environment young people face as opposed to trying to categorize them all into boxes and identities that don't fit very well and are constantly shifting, you give yourself a fighting chance to truly understand their world and be empathetic toward the pressures and realities they face. You can listen better, show up more authentically, and help them see the way that their faith and spiritual lives intersect with all these things.

Furthermore, this focus gives you a foothold on something you can actually control and shape. Once you understand the types of situations young people are in, you can influence, alter, and change those situations or the responses and choices that young people perceive in those situations. You can create conditions that lead to greater belonging. You can leverage the low-trust tools of relationships to connect more effectively with young people. You can reimagine faith as a journey with a trusted guide as opposed to a singular destination. Social media can become a setting for faith and values to be explored and lived out.

You have a distinct and important role to play in all that as a faith leader, and young people need you in those spaces. They affirm time and again in both formal studies and informal comments that they really, really want adults to help them navigate and make sense of all these pressures. In the coming chapters, we'll dive deeper into each of these topics and give you some specific tools to use that might help you do your work along the way.

SACRED SNAPSHOTS:
Engaging Youth in Visual Testimony

Introduction

The process of engaging youth in defining and sharing their spiritual landscapes is not just beneficial for their individual growth; it also promotes a richer, more inclusive understanding within the faith community. Photovoice is a participatory research method that empowers individuals to use photography and narrative to document, reflect on, and communicate their experiences and perspectives. In this tool, we use it to help young people articulate their sacred experiences, thereby fostering a culture of shared understanding and respect. This activity is designed to enhance relational ministry by providing an expressive platform for youth and promoting intergenerational dialogue.

This activity utilizes the photovoice methodology, which has emerged as a dynamic tool for empowerment and expression, especially for youth and other populations that are often marginalized.[1] It allows them to capture and communicate their perspectives through photography, leading to profound community and self-engagement.[2]

---

1. For more about how photovoice can be used in faith settings, please see the remarkable work of Dr. Roman Williams and Interfaith Photovoice (https://interfaithphotovoice.org/).

2. Robert W. Strack, Cathleen Magill, and Kara McDonagh, "Engaging Youth Through Photovoice," *Health Promotion Practice* 5, no. 1 (January 2004): 49–58, https://doi.org/10.1177/1524839903258015.

Recognizing the versatility of this medium, congregations can apply photovoice to help young members articulate their spiritual experiences, as it offers a unique window into the interplay between spirituality and everyday life.

Objectives

- Provide youth with a medium to express their spirituality visually.
- Create a space for intergenerational dialogue through shared experiences.
- Deepen understanding of teenage spirituality within the community.
- Foster enduring relationships through the shared exploration of what is considered sacred.

Pre-Activity Preparations

Materials Needed

- Digital cameras or smartphones
- Printer for physical copies
- Digital tools for online display (e.g., slideshow program, social media platform)

Setup

- Arrange for a workshop to discuss the concept of sacredness.
- Prepare a display area for the final exhibition.
- Ensure availability of photography resources.

Step 1: Set the Intention (*Imago Dei*)

Before beginning, take a few moments to establish the purpose of this exercise with the group. Remind participants that Sacred Listening starts with recognizing the divine in each person. Explain that every interaction is sacred, and the images they capture are not just photos but reflections of their personal experiences and connection to the community.

Share that this exercise is about seeing and listening—truly seeing one another's lives and listening to the stories behind the images. This exercise is an invitation to view one another as sacred, honoring the unique stories we each carry.

Suggested introduction: "We are embarking on a journey today where the pictures you take will help us see the world through your eyes. This isn't just about taking photos; it's about capturing moments that express who you are and where you belong. Let's remember that each person's story is sacred."

Step 2: Capture Moments (Alignment)

Next, give participants time to capture images that reflect the themes of "expressions of joy" or "places of belonging." Encourage them to interpret these themes freely, as Sacred Listening emphasizes alignment—the idea that each person expresses their reality differently. This is about letting participants communicate in a way that resonates with them, whether through capturing people, places, or objects that symbolize belonging.

Participants can use cameras, smartphones, or any available device to take pictures that represent their personal experiences of joy or belonging. The images might reflect a physical place, a group of people, or even a symbolic object.

Example prompts:

- What makes you feel connected to others?
- What places or moments make you feel at home?
- What image represents joy in your life?

These prompts are designed to guide participants in choosing images that are meaningful to them.

Step 3: Share and Reflect (Pattern Recognition)

Once everyone has had time to capture their photos, gather the group back together to share their images. During this time, encourage participants to explain why they chose each image and what it represents to them. As others listen, they are practicing Sacred Listening by being present and open to the experiences being shared.

Facilitate the sharing process by prompting participants with open-ended questions that encourage deeper reflection. Ask questions like

- What story does this image tell about your experience?
- How does this photo reflect your sense of belonging?
- What do you want us to understand about your perspective from this image?

As participants share, take notes or invite a designated notetaker to write down key insights or themes that emerge. This act of recording reinforces that what participants share matters and will be remembered.

After the initial sharing of images, shift the conversation to explore common themes or patterns that emerge from the stories shared. This step connects to the pattern recognition principle of Sacred Listening, where the focus is on not just individual stories but broader connections within the group.

Guide a discussion around the themes that have emerged. For example,

- Did you notice any common threads in the stories or images we've seen?
- How do these photos collectively represent our community's experience of belonging?
- What new perspectives or insights have you gained from seeing the world through someone else's eyes?

Encourage reflection. This discussion helps participants connect their individual experiences to the larger group, fostering a sense of shared understanding and deeper connection.

Step 4: Extending Relationships (Scaling Up, Out, and Down)

Finally, Sacred Listening doesn't stop with the conversation. Encourage participants to think about how these stories and images can continue to shape their understanding of belonging and community. Plan future activities that build on the insights gained during this session, ensuring that the relationships and conversations continue to grow.

The follow-up phase of this exercise maps directly onto scaling up, out, and down in ministry:

- Scaling up: Use the themes from the photos and stories to inform broader ministry strategies. Insights gathered can shape programming or communications that speak to a larger audience while still feeling personal and targeted.
- Scaling out: Share the photos and insights with volunteers or small-group leaders, empowering them to engage with participants and their stories. This allows the relational work to spread across the community, decentralizing the responsibility for follow-up.
- Scaling down: Identify participants who shared particularly meaningful or vulnerable stories. Follow up individually with them to deepen those connections quickly, fostering trust and spiritual growth in a focused and intentional way.

Summarize the key themes that emerged and propose follow-up actions or future gatherings on the basis of these insights. For example,

- Organize a gallery walk where participants display their photos for a larger audience, inviting further reflection and conversation.
- Plan future photo challenges where participants can explore new themes, deepening their connection to one another over time.
- Invite participants to continue reflecting on the themes of joy and belonging in their everyday lives and share new images at the next gathering.

Example of future planning: "As we reflect on the themes that emerged today, let's think about how we can continue this conversation. What new themes might we explore next? How can these insights help us build an even stronger sense of community?"

Conclusion

This photovoice project transcends mere activity; it is a strategic initiative to cultivate understanding and connection within the faith community. By involving both youth and adults in a visual testimony of sacredness, we pave the way for a culture of empathy and inclusivity, ensuring that the ministry remains connected and relevant to all its members.

FAITH IS A CONVERSATION

Summer Camp

When I was in college, I worked at Sky Ranch Lutheran Camp in Colorado. My job was to lead young people to a mountaintop experience on an actual mountaintop. It was amazing. I can still vividly recall those Sunday afternoons when campers would arrive for the week. The buses and vans rolled into camp, and groups of kids would stumble out the doors in sweatpants and hoodies, their legs weary from sitting for hours and their eyes wide open from the breathtaking vistas they saw on the way up the mountain.

The altitude was also literally breathtaking, and watching them struggle to breathe at ten thousand feet after jogging more than a few yards never failed to amuse. Never mind that the leaders had been in their exact same position, gasping for air, just a few weeks before when we arrived for training. The adults driving the vehicles were also breathless, but that probably had more to do with the white-knuckle road leading up to the camp than anything else.

Even though staff weren't required to be there right when the campers got off the bus, I always wanted to be there. I learned early on that I could get a sense of what my week was going to be like just by watching those first few moments.

Would they be laughing and hugging and still in conversations full of inside jokes that had clearly been going on for hours? Or would they be quiet, headphones on, unsure, and timid? So much of what I was going to be able to do that week depended not on my training and ability but on the community they had with one another before they ever set foot at camp.

It took me years of research and conversations, though, to understand that the insight I had about that moment was only half the equation. I wanted to watch them get off the bus, because I thought if I could better understand how they came to me at that moment, then I could serve them better and get them to where they needed to be in their faith by the end of the week. Chalk it up to the pride of youth.

For the groups that were disconnected and disaffected, I would try to be the dynamic camp counselor that they could all center on. For the ones rolling in with a community intact, I would try to figure out who the leaders were and channel that energy into the activities of the week.

But the end goal was the same. I wanted to change hearts and deepen conviction. I wanted them to experience and know God so certainly that they would make a commitment and never waver. And I have to say, it really seemed to work.

By the time they left on Friday afternoon, I would, more often than not, be able to sleep well, thinking that I had made a real, lasting difference in their lives. They would be going home as changed people primed to make an important impact on their local communities and friend groups forever.

Oh, how wrong I was.

It's not that camp and mountaintop experiences aren't important. They definitely are. But what I failed to understand was their particular kind of importance. I thought that if I could elicit an intense enough experience, I would get an equally intense commitment from them. Back then I thought faith was like a bucket. I thought if I could fill up their faith bucket enough, then it could never empty.

But that's just not true. The reality is that young people don't experience faith and spirituality in this way. Young people see faith as part of the general development of their lives (if they think about faith at all) rather than as a box to be checked or a switch to be activated. Similarly to all the other areas of development, there are times when their faith life is more salient and important and times when it just isn't top of mind for them.

Rather than filling up their bucket, I should have been showing them how to go to the well when they needed it. I would have been better off helping them cultivate good skills for asking questions of the right people and listening for truth rather than trying to get them to arrive at a particular understanding. What young people need are the skills to enter into the "conversation" of faith that can last them a lifetime.

Metallica and Baseball

The big lesson that I've learned in the twenty-five years since I was a camp counselor actually didn't come from any data or research. Instead, it came from a simple question that a college student asked me after I had given a talk early in my career. He wanted to know if I had always wanted to be a professor.

"No," I replied. "For the longest time I wanted to be an NFL quarterback or center fielder for the Texas Rangers. I was an undeclared major until my college refused to let me enroll in any more classes unless I made a decision. So I picked English since I had the most credits accumulated there already. After college I went into AmeriCorps in Washington, DC, and volunteered for some public policy organizations while there before ultimately landing in graduate school for sociology."

In other words, when I was a teenager and in my early twenties, I certainly did not aspire to be a professor or a researcher in any way, even though I was very grateful to have the opportunity as an adult.

This simple question got me thinking about young people in a new and different way. How many of us are doing the things that we dreamed for ourselves when we were thirteen, fourteen, or fifteen years old? I'm not married to the girl I was dating in high school. I don't live where I thought I would live. I don't drive the car I lusted after. In fact, my life now looks different in nearly every material way than I would have imagined as a teenager. And that's all for the better, I might add. My teenage self had some very odd aspirations.

I suspect the same is true for most of you as well. Sometimes when I give talks and want to make this point, I ask the audience to close their eyes and recall themselves in their childhood bedroom. What posters are on the wall? What music is playing? What are they wearing?

Then we open our eyes and share our answers before I ask one more set of questions. Who is still wearing those same clothes? Who was listening to that music in the car on the way over here? Who has those same posters on their walls?

The answer, of course, is that very, very few of us are the same in any real, substantive way as we were when we were young. It doesn't mean that our values have radically changed, but the expression of them almost always has.

It would be comical to meet a forty-five-year-old adult who acts the same as they did when they were fifteen. Perhaps you know a few!

We understand intuitively that youth is a time for exploring, experimenting, trying on new identities, and finding passions, causes, and vocations that allow us to channel our values, beliefs, and commitments into a unique expression of ourselves in the world.

And the science backs up our idea of youth as a time of exploration. Research in various fields of psychology, sociology, and neuroscience supports the idea that it is normal for young people to explore different identities, careers, beliefs, and more. These studies shed light on the developmental processes that occur during adolescence and early adulthood, highlighting the significance of exploration and self-discovery during this period.

According to psychologist Erik Erikson's theory of psychosocial development, individuals go through a stage called "identity versus role confusion" during their teenage years.[1] This stage is charac-

---

1. Erik H. Erikson, *Identity: Youth and Crisis* (Norton, 1968).

terized by the exploration of different roles, values, and beliefs as adolescents strive to establish a sense of self and determine their place in society. It is during this time that young people actively experiment with different identities, trying on various personas to understand what resonates with their authentic selves.

Social scientists who study work and occupations tend to take a different approach but come to a similar conclusion.[2] They emphasize the importance of exploration in shaping one's career path and life choices. The concept of career construction suggests that individuals construct their careers through a series of choices and experiences rather than following a linear trajectory. The exploration of different occupational possibilities, interests, and skills allows young people to gain a deeper understanding of their strengths and passions. This process of career exploration helps individuals make informed decisions about their future and align their work with their personal values and aspirations.

Brain scientists offer yet more support.[3] Neuroscience research has provided insights into the changes in the brain that occur during adolescence that contribute to exploratory behavior. The prefrontal cortex, responsible for decision-making and self-regulation, undergoes significant development during this period. This maturation enables young people to engage in more complex cognitive processes, think critically, and consider different perspectives. It also facilitates the capacity for introspection and self-reflection, encouraging individuals to question their beliefs and seek new experiences.

Additionally, exposure to diverse experiences and viewpoints during youth promotes cognitive flexibility and adaptability.[4] By

2. M. L. Savickas, "The Theory and Practice of Career Construction," in *Career Development and Counseling: Putting Theory and Research to Work*, ed. S. D. Brown and R. W. Lent (Wiley & Sons, 2005).

3. Laurence Steinberg, "Cognitive and Affective Development in Adolescence," *Trends in Cognitive Sciences* 9, no. 2 (2005): 69–74, https://doi.org/10.1016/j.tics.2004.12.005.

4. William Damon, *The Path to Purpose: How Young People Find Their Calling in Life* (Free Press, 2008).

exploring various identities, careers, and beliefs, young people broaden their horizons, challenge assumptions, and develop a more nuanced understanding of the world. This process of exploration fosters personal growth, empathy, and a greater appreciation for diversity.

In other words, the science is pretty unanimous that adolescence is, as mentioned above, a time of exploration, experimentation, and a kind of "trying on" of different identities, roles, and activities. And not only do scientists agree that these things typically occur during adolescence; they also make it pretty clear that the evidence shows that it's good for us to be exposed to new ideas and ways of living during this time of life.

But you probably don't need science to know all that. You've lived it. If you've been working with young people for any length of time, you've even seen this development take place. Not only do we understand that adolescence is a time of exploration, but we also often support and encourage it as normal and healthy.

Except when it comes to faith.

When it comes to religion and faith and spirituality it's like we forget everything we know about young people. We suspend our reality long enough to think that if we can just shelter them from influences we don't agree with and make sure they are really, really steeped in our own religious tradition, then they'll never stray, never doubt. If we can just fill up their bucket enough, they'll never explore. But that's just not the case.

Religious Identity Formation

Given that so much of adolescence is about exploration, it should come as no surprise that young people take this same approach to their religious and spiritual lives. Just as they experiment with different identities, careers, and beliefs, adolescents often engage in a period of exploration and questioning when it comes to matters of religion.

Research in the field of religious studies and developmental psychology highlights the dynamic nature of religious and spiritual beliefs during youth.⁵ Adolescence is a time when individuals begin to question the beliefs and values they were raised with, seeking to develop a personal understanding of their spirituality. This process, known as "religious identity formation," involves exploring various religious traditions, engaging in philosophical discussions, and reflecting on personal experiences.

In many cultures, adolescence is seen as a transitional period, and young individuals are often encouraged to explore different religious perspectives. This exploration is considered essential for them to establish their own sense of faith and spiritual connection. It allows young people to evaluate their beliefs, examine alternative worldviews, and determine what resonates with their evolving understanding of the world and their place within it.⁶

Moreover, studies have shown that religious exploration during adolescence is associated with positive outcomes, such as increased empathy, tolerance, and critical thinking skills. When young people engage in an open-minded exploration of different religious and spiritual traditions, they gain a broader perspective on diverse belief systems and cultural practices. This exposure fosters intercultural understanding, respect, and appreciation for religious diversity.⁷

It is worth noting that the research also shows that the exploration of religion does not necessarily imply a rejection of one's previous beliefs or traditions. Rather, it represents a natural process of self-discovery and growth. Many young people may find that their exploration leads them to reaffirm their faith or adopt a more nuanced understanding of their religious beliefs. For others, it may involve transitioning to a different religious tradition, adopting a spiritual but nonreligious worldview, or embracing agnosticism or atheism.

---

5. P. E. King and C. J. Boyatzis, "Religious and Spiritual Development," in *Handbook of Child Psychology and Developmental Science*, vol. 3, *Socioemotional Processes*, 7th ed., ed. M. E. Lamb and R. M. Lerner (Wiley & Sons, 2015).

6. King and Boyatzis, "Religious and Spiritual Development."

7. P. E. King and R. W. Roeser, "Religion and Spirituality in Adolescent Development," in *Handbook of Parenting*, vol. 1, *Children and Parenting*, 3rd ed., ed. Marc H. Bornstein (Routledge, 2019).

Recognizing and supporting the exploration of religion and spirituality during adolescence is crucial for fostering a healthy and authentic religious life. Encouraging young people to ask questions, engage in dialogue, and explore different religious perspectives can empower them to develop a meaningful and personally relevant spiritual framework. This exploration allows them to integrate their values, ethics, and beliefs into their evolving identities, contributing to their overall well-being and sense of purpose.

Why do we think religion is different from the other areas of a young person's life? It's sort of silly when you stop and think about it. We act as if change is the hallmark of youth for everything, except the most important thing. If I don't drive the car that I dreamed about as a fifteen-year-old, and I'm only occasionally listening to the band that I thought was the best thing ever in middle school (Metallica), and I actually *didn't* grow up to play center field for my beloved Texas Rangers, it shouldn't really come as any surprise that my own faith at forty-five is markedly different than it was at fifteen.

> We act as if change is the hallmark of youth for everything, except the most important thing.

I suspect yours is too.

I wandered through countless expressions on my religious journey while seeking an understanding of the most important force in my life. I wasn't a dilettante or lacking in faithfulness just because I was asking questions and seeing how other religious traditions operated. I wasn't doing something aberrant or abnormal. In fact, I was doing exactly what teenagers are supposed to do with the things that are most important to them.

Conversation, Not Oration

A few years ago I interviewed a young person about her faith journey, and she gave a ten-minute answer defending moral and spiritual relativism. The content was not at all surprising for anyone who listens to a lot of young people talk about faith and religion. Thankfully, it was recorded.

When I play this recorded answer for people, they sometimes grow very concerned about how she could combine parts and pieces from very different religious traditions into a hodgepodge. They sometimes call her shallow and claim that she exhibits the kind of weak faith that we need to correct in young people. They want to catechize her more, make her attend church more, and put her through confirmation or religious education classes. They want to fill up her bucket with more information, the *right* information.

But what those adults miss is the bigger picture. They're focused on the content of the answer when they should be focusing on the fact that she can give a well-considered, ten-minute answer about her faith journey at all. In other words, she's taking this aspect of her life very, very seriously. She has clearly put a lot of intentional time and effort into this exploration. This indicates a level of commitment and ownership that will last a lifetime even as the particulars of her faith and spirituality change.

The adults are concerned about the content because they think her content is the outcome. Even though they know all the things about teenagers we just covered above, they fall right into the trap of forgetting about the earnest importance of exploration for young people. Instead of focusing on how much she knows about God and religion, they should be far more concerned about how she's getting her information. What sources does she use to experience the divine? Who is she listening to?

We should be far, far more concerned about whether young people can offer age-appropriate explanations of their beliefs and journeys than we should be about whether they give the "right" answers. We know only one thing for certain about young people: They're going to change. The real question is how. And when they're ready to ask questions, who will be there to guide them?

This is what I missed as a camp counselor. I couldn't give them an intense enough experience to stave off exploration or questions or doubt because there isn't a mountaintop high enough or a bucket big enough for that sort of thing.

That is simply not how young people are equipped, biologically or socially, to behave with the things they're most serious about. Religion, belief, faith, and spirituality for young people are no longer based on the rote memorization of fundamental theological truths (if they ever were). They're based on the right questions and understanding how the answers fit together. This doesn't mean that we have to abandon the idea that there *is* a right answer, but it does mean that we need to get a little more comfortable with the journey.

Less oration and more conversation.

Let me explain how this has changed just in our lifetimes. When my father was growing up, his dad managed department stores. If you're of a certain age, you can conjure an image of the stand-alone department store that had everything you would need under one roof. Sometimes, these stores took up whole city blocks. My dad once told me that when he went back-to-school shopping, he could get whatever style of clothes he wanted—so long as they had it in the store. Essentially, it was a take-it-or-leave-it proposition. Not much choice.

It was the same for his faith. He grew up Catholic in a Catholic neighborhood and went to Catholic schools. He could believe or not believe. That was really the only choice.

By the time I was a teenager, the options had expanded a bit. The stand-alone department store model had died for the most part, and I spent hours shopping at the mall with every kind of shop I could imagine. The analogy to my faith is clear. I was at least *aware* that there were different options to explore. The internet, where any topic could be explored, was coming into existence, and my own excellent public school education exposed me to the different major belief systems in the world.

Although I had never been to a mosque, synagogue, or temple and couldn't name any non-Christians that I personally knew, I was aware that they existed. At some theoretical level, I was also aware that I could *be* Christian or Jewish or Buddhist or anything else. Just like shopping at a mall gave me real choices, though my clothes weren't tailor-made, religion was no longer a take-it-or-leave-it proposition.

Today's young people would find both of those situations ridiculous. They have Amazon, Etsy, and the entire internet available for their shopping needs. There is very little, from the mass-produced to the bespoke, that they can't buy in just a few clicks. And the same is true of their faith. There are so many more choices to be made in every aspect of their lives. Young people today live in a world of unlimited choice, and the data show that this extends to how they encounter religion and spirituality as well.

Young people in America today are increasingly becoming religious explorers, a trend that reflects the shifting landscape of faith and spirituality. According to data from the Pew Research Center, a substantial number of young adults—particularly millennials—are reshaping the religious panorama with their varied quest for spiritual meaning.[8] PRRI further corroborates this with findings that highlight the fluidity of religious identity among younger generations, showing their notable willingness to cross traditional boundaries in search of a faith that resonates with their individual beliefs and experiences.[9]

Gallup's tracking of religious attitudes and affiliations complements this picture, indicating that a significant portion of young people are open to changing their religious affiliation or lack thereof, suggesting a pattern of ongoing spiritual and religious experimentation and discovery.[10] This evidence points to a dynamic and evolving domain of religious engagement, where exploration is often the hallmark of young people's spiritual journeys.

These data aren't in our favor if we're expecting young people to simply replicate the decisions of past generations. When young people live in a world of infinite choices, nothing is going to keep

---

8. "When Americans Say They Believe in God, What Do They Mean?," Pew Research Center, April 25, 2018, https://www.pewforum.org/2018/04/25/when-americans-say-they-believe-in-god-what-do-they-mean/.

9. Daniel Cox and Robert P. Jones, "America's Changing Religious Identity," PRRI, September 6, 2017, https://www.prri.org/research/american-religious-landscape-christian-religiously-unaffiliated/.

10. Jeffrey M. Jones, "U.S. Church Membership Falls Below Majority for First Time," Gallup, March 29, 2021, https://news.gallup.com/poll/341963/church-membership-falls-below-majority-first-time.aspx.

them from exploring. Our job now is to show them how to navigate those choices, not to try and restrict them from making them.

Sleep Poorly

But I understand how tempting it is just to tell them what to do. When I reflected on my days as a camp counselor years after they were over, I realized that what I was doing with young people was essentially making myself feel better.

I went to sleep at night convinced that I had spoken truth to them. Even when I had doubts about my own ability, at least I knew I had done my best to convince them of the importance of faith. But that was really about me, not them. I slept better, but I'm not so sure that they got what they really needed.

So I get it. If we commit to helping young people ask the right questions and find trusted adults who can guide them and accompany them on the exploration, we won't sleep well. In fact, we'll go to bed each night wondering if we should have done more or pushed harder. It'll feel like we're doing less if we don't take every moment to proclaim and convince young people about the capital-*T* Truth.

We feel uniquely responsible for all their religious and spiritual outcomes, but we don't have to. As Christians, we operate inside a system that explicitly requires acknowledgment of a God who moves and operates through the Holy Spirit in this world.

We don't have to do everything. Yes, the stakes are high. We're talking about the eternal souls of young people that we care about

> As Christians, we operate inside a system that explicitly requires acknowledgment of a God who moves and operates through the Holy Spirit in this world. We don't have to do everything.

very deeply, not to mention the health of the church as an institution. But you can't do it all. And you're not expected to.

Supporting Exploration

Fortunately, there are specific activities we can undertake to support a teenager's religious development and contribute to a deeper faith commitment as an adult.

First, facilitating open discussions and exploring religious texts together can be highly beneficial. Research suggests that engaging in dialogue and studying religious scriptures as a family or community helps foster critical thinking and a deeper understanding of faith. Parents and adults can encourage a thoughtful exploration of beliefs by creating a safe space where teenagers can freely express their thoughts and ask questions about religious teachings.[11] We should keep in mind that encouraging young people to ask questions does not imply that they need answers or that we have to provide them.

The act of formulating a question is a valuable end in itself. While it can be hard to not immediately provide an answer when we feel like we have one, consider answering their question with another question or directed statement. Perhaps the most powerful tool a trusted adult has is the statement "That's really interesting; tell me more about that." If the goal is to get young people to engage in serious, deep thought about their religious lives and beliefs, then we should be trying to foster more reflection rather than trying to get to the right destination as quickly as possible.

Second, fostering mentorship and providing spiritual guidance are important. Mentorship plays a significant role in shaping religious identity and commitment among adolescents. Mentors cannot take the place of parents, but it is helpful for young people to have a trusted adult that they can ask questions they might not feel comfortable asking their parents right away. We often try out

---

11. Eugene C. Roehlkepartain, Pamela Ebstyne King, Linda Wagener, and Peter L. Benson, eds., *The Handbook of Spiritual Development in Childhood and Adolescence* (SAGE, 2006).

> Perhaps the most powerful tool a trusted adult has is the statement "That's really interesting; tell me more about that." . . . We should be trying to foster more reflection rather than trying to get to the right destination as quickly as possible.

questions or explorations with people who pose low social risk before we start communicating those questions to others.

In this way, mentors can serve as a staging ground, or a place to audition exploration. However, they should never be seen as substitutes for parents or caregivers, who are the ones who ultimately need to have these conversations with their teenagers. Connecting teenagers with mentors or spiritual leaders who exemplify a deep and sincere faith commitment can provide invaluable guidance, inspiration, and support on their spiritual journey.

Finally, engaging in community service and outreach activities is another powerful way to support religious development.[12] Participation in community service aligned with religious values fosters a sense of purpose, compassion, and moral development. As I mentioned above, we should be helping young people understand how to engage in the "conversation" of faith rather than just trying to get them to memorize the "right" answers.

Showing teenagers how to practice faith will give them a fundamental skill they need to develop their own faith. If they have enough of these experiences and practice, then as they grow and mature, they should be able to put their faith into action to answer whether their beliefs have any impact in the world. In addition,

---

12. Pamela Ebstyne King and James L. Furrow, "Religion as a Resource for Positive Youth Development: Religion, Social Capital, and Moral Outcomes," *Developmental Psychology* 40, no. 5 (2004): 703–13.

service helps strengthen the core components of any faith system and forces people to grapple with what religious commitment means for their own lives.

Furniture and Faith: The IKEA Effect

A few years ago, my wife and I decided to tackle the daunting task of assembling an IKEA bookshelf together. We carefully followed the instructions and YouTube tutorials, deciphered the diagrams, and spent hours laboring over every screw and bolt with those tiny tools provided in the kit. Surprisingly, as we completed the final step and stood back to admire our handiwork, a sense of pride washed over us. It wasn't just any furniture; it was something we had put together with our own hands. We cherished that piece more than any other, even those that were family heirlooms made of solid oak (don't tell Grandma!).

It's incredibly irrational on its surface. Why would particleboard and nearly idiotproof assembly instructions result in a sense of pride? After all, we probably could have just spent a little bit more money and bought the furniture already assembled. If we had done that, we could have easily ended up with a living room full of the exact same furniture—but we would have far less commitment to it or pride in it.

Instead, we moved that flimsy bookshelf from one apartment to the next in graduate school and then from one house to another when we got real jobs. Today, it still lives on in our basement, holding overflow books and photo albums. It has survived all these years not because it's the most beautiful thing ever but because we took so much pride in having built it that it just became a part of our lives.

Interestingly, this phenomenon has been studied and is known as "the IKEA effect," coined by researchers Michael Norton, Daniel Mochon, and Dan Ariely.[13] The IKEA effect is the tendency for

13. Michael I. Norton, Daniel Mochon, and Dan Ariely, "The IKEA Effect: When Labor Leads to Love," *Journal of Consumer Psychology* 22, no. 3 (2012): 453–60.

individuals to assign greater value and attachment to objects they have actively participated in creating or assembling. It's a psychological phenomenon that highlights the satisfaction and sense of ownership that comes from personal involvement.

The IKEA effect helps explain why a little bit of what designers and user-experience experts call "friction" is actually beneficial for end users. If things are *too* easy or prepackaged and ready to go, then we tend to think of them as disposable. The minute it doesn't work or fit into our lives, we just think we can toss it and get another one. A little bit of friction from participating in part of something's creation increases short-term frustration a little bit but sets people up for long-term investment.

Just as my wife and I took pride in the furniture we built, individuals who have explored and crafted their own faith often feel a stronger sense of ownership over their beliefs and values. By allowing teenagers to embark on their own journey of religious exploration, we provide them with the opportunity to build their faith from the ground up. They can actively engage in asking questions, seeking answers, and forming their own understanding of spirituality.

Encouraging teenagers to explore and craft their own faith lives doesn't mean abandoning them or neglecting guidance. On the contrary, it means accompanying them as trusted adults, being present to support their exploration, and providing a safe space for them to question, reflect, and develop their unique spiritual perspectives.

Research consistently demonstrates that when teenagers take ownership of their faith, it transforms into a deeply personal and meaningful aspect of their lives. A study conducted by Christian Smith and Patricia Snell found that adolescents who actively participated in shaping their religious beliefs reported higher levels of religious commitment and satisfaction compared with those whose faith was primarily dictated by external factors.[14] Along

---

14. Christian Smith and Patricia Snell, *Souls in Transition: The Religious and Spiritual Lives of Emerging Adults* (Oxford University Press, 2009).

those same lines, Eugene Roehlkepartain and colleagues highlight that adolescents who perceive their faith as a personal choice rather than an imposed obligation are more likely to experience a sense of purpose, internalize moral values, and engage in religious practices throughout their lives.[15]

Perhaps most importantly, data indicate that a sense of ownership and a personal investment in faith during teenage years are more likely to lead to continued religious practice and participation as an adult.[16] While it might take longer than just getting a faith or belief system off the shelf, it will be more deeply held, more durable, and more likely to stick with them well into adulthood.

So let us, as parents and adults, embark on the courageous path of supporting teenagers in their exploration of the divine, trusting that their journey of self-discovery will lead to a deeper and more genuine commitment than any amount of persuasion ever could.

---

15. Roehlkepartain et al., *Handbook of Spiritual Development*.
16. Christian Smith and Melinda Lundquist Denton, *Soul Searching: The Religious and Spiritual Lives of American Teenagers* (Oxford University Press, 2005).

THE QUESTION-WALL TOOL:
A Step-by-Step Guide for Youth Ministers

Introduction

The IKEA effect, mentioned above, tells us that young people are more likely to develop a deep and lasting connection to their spiritual and faith lives when they actively participate in constructing their beliefs and ideas instead of passively accepting prepackaged religious doctrines by seeking opportunities to engage in critical conversations and shape their own faith journeys.

In a society where questions often go unasked or unanswered, fostering a space where young people can freely inquire about their spiritual and existential concerns is crucial.

Objectives

- Allow young people to articulate their own questions and concerns.
- Facilitate group discussion and reflection.
- Create a repository of questions to guide future activities and discussions.
- Help build connections among various age groups within your faith community to scale your relational ministry.

SACRED LISTENING TOOL

Pre-Activity Preparations

Materials Needed
- Large poster board
- Markers
- Post-its in different colors (one color per participant if possible)
- Pens or pencils
- Timer or stopwatch
- Journal or paper for reflection
- Notecards

Setup
- Hang the poster board in an easily accessible location.
- Write the following headings somewhere on the poster board. Feel free to alter the headings or come up with different ones related to faith, religion, and spirituality that suit your community. Make sure to leave ample space around each for Post-its:
  - Spirituality
  - Religious teachings
  - Meaning/purpose
  - The church
  - Other

Step 1: Set the Intention (*Imago Dei*)

Begin by centering the group with a moment of reflection on the sacredness of each person. Frame the question-wall exercise as an opportunity to honor the divine in one another by creating a space where every question is valuable and every voice is heard. Let participants know that their questions are not meant to be answered right away but are an important part of their faith journey.

Share with the group that asking questions is a sacred act and that they are creating a space where curiosity and reflection are embraced as part of spiritual growth. Consider reading a passage, quote, or poem that emphasizes the value of asking questions.

Step 2: Ask and Record (Alignment)

When people are tasked with thinking about very abstract things, it's helpful to give them some concrete boundaries. The constraints will help focus and balance out the nature of the task. One way to provide boundaries is to use a structure called "five in three," which requires participants to come up with five questions in three minutes. Reassure them that these don't have to be the five most important questions in their life. They just need five. As a reminder, these are not questions that require answers. The point of this exercise is to see the commonality in the questions.

The participants should write down their questions on Post-its and place them on a large poster- or whiteboard under specific categories, such as "spirituality," "religious teachings," "purpose," and "the church." This aligns with the Sacred Listening principle of meeting people where they are by allowing them to express their doubts, concerns, or curiosity in a way that feels safe and open-ended.

Phase 1. Use the five-in-three method, where participants write five questions in three minutes. Encourage participants to be open and spontaneous, reminding them that there are no right or wrong questions.

Phase 2. For some people it can be freeing to ask questions as if they were someone else. It feels safer and helps generate a wider array of questions. This persona exercise, adapted from the good people at CoCreative (https://www.wearecocreative.com), helps generate more questions in a safe environment. Introduce the concept of personas. Explain that everyone will now be asking questions as if they were someone else. Provide a list of personas and encourage the participants to add additional personas they think would be useful: my pastor, the pope, my grandmother or grandfather, Olivia Rodrigo, my best friend, Lil Nas X, Florence Pugh, Greta Thunberg, Billie Eilish, my significant other, Taylor Swift, or my favorite teacher/coach/mentor. Repeat the five-in-three approach from above, but make sure they know to note which persona they're writing from on their sticky note. Have them place their questions on the wall in the right category.

Step 3: Share and Reflect (Pattern Recognition)

After the questions are posted, the group will gather around the question wall to recognize patterns and group similar questions together. This step is about recognizing shared concerns and showing participants that they are not alone in their questions. Reflecting on the common themes allows for a deeper understanding of the group's spiritual landscape.

Guide the group through the process of identifying overlapping themes and patterns. Ask open-ended questions like

- What themes are emerging in the questions you've posted?
- Do any of these questions resonate with you personally?

Facilitate discussion as participants move questions around and reflect on the emerging groupings. Encourage them to see that they are not alone in their questions, fostering a sense of belonging and shared curiosity.

Once the questions have been shared and grouped, lead the group in a deeper conversation about the questions that stood out the most. Encourage participants to reflect on how it feels to see their own questions alongside others' and what they've learned from the experience.

Facilitate a brief journaling session where participants can write about one or two questions that sparked the most reflection. Then, invite volunteers to share their reflections with the group.

Potential prompts for journaling or discussion include

- How did it feel to see your questions next to others'?
- What do these questions say about our community's shared spiritual journey?

Step 4: Extending Relationships (Scaling Up, Out, and Down)

The follow-up for the question-wall exercise helps scale relationships up, out, and down, ensuring that the questions and connections generated continue to shape ministry.

- Scaling up: After the exercise, capture all the questions in a tracking sheet or digital document. Organize them by theme or category, tagging each with the participant's name and the date. Use these insights to guide future group discussions, sermon topics, or programming decisions that reflect the needs and questions of your community.
- Scaling out: Share the questions with other leaders or ministry teams. Encourage them to repeat this exercise with different groups, such as parents or adult congregants, using the questions to bridge generational divides. The tracking sheet can help identify common questions or concerns that could foster deeper intergenerational dialogue and engagement.
- Scaling down: Use the tracking sheet to identify individual participants who may benefit from further one-on-one follow-up. For example, if someone raised a particularly vulnerable or deep question, consider reaching out to them personally to offer continued conversation or spiritual guidance. This individualized follow-up deepens relationships more quickly by addressing specific needs.

By capturing the information in a tracking sheet and scaling the exercise up, out, and down, you will ensure that the questions don't just sit on the wall but become an active part of your ministry's ongoing efforts to foster trust, connection, and spiritual growth.

3

A DISAFFILIATED WORLD

Measure What Matters

If you looked at movie rentals and ticket sales at theaters in 1995, you'd have a pretty good sense of how much people were interested in movies. But if you were to look at those same two metrics today, you'd come to the conclusion that in the past twenty-five years people have really started to hate watching movies and that maybe movie watching was just a fad that has run its course and is now going the way of the dodo bird.

But that would be the wrong conclusion, of course. The reality is that today, people consume just as many, if not more, movies as they ever have. The market research firm Statista found that in 2021, during the pandemic, nearly one-third of eighteen-to-forty-four-year-olds watched movies every day![1] Of course, they weren't going to theaters; they were streaming. The decline in ticket sales and rentals isn't because we stopped watching movies. It's simply that we're watching movies in different ways than we used to, and

---

1. Julia Stoll, "Frequency of Watching or Streaming Movies Among Adults in the United States as of September 2021, by Age Group," Statista, January 12, 2023, https://www.statista.com/statistics/935493/movies-watching-streaming-frequency-us-by-age/.

traditional metrics like ticket sales and rental revenue don't capture the full picture anymore.

This is sort of how it works with the world of religion. For the longest time we relied on just a handful of key indicators to tell us how interested people were in church. We tracked statistics like attendance, giving, and membership to drive our assessment of overall religiosity. Many of us still do.

When we compare those numbers today with those of thirty, forty, or fifty years ago, what we find is alarming.

In the 1950s just over 70 percent of Americans were members of a local congregation. Today that number is around 45 percent.[2]

People with no religious affiliation (a.k.a., Nones) made up 5 percent of the population in the 1970s and account for 30 percent of the adult population today and for well over one-third of Gen Z. At the same time, the number of people who identified as "Christian" held steady at around 90 percent of the population throughout the 1970s, '80s, and '90s, but it now sits around 65 percent.[3]

Donations to congregations and religious organizations, which accounted for nearly 60 percent of all charitable giving in the early 1980s, now make up just 27 percent of donations, according to Giving USA.[4]

None of this happened overnight. Just as the shift from theaters to rentals to streaming wasn't like flipping a light switch, the move away from institutional religion has not been abrupt. Instead, it's been a steady softening.[5] Every year, the traditional metrics of

---

2. Jeffrey M. Jones, "U.S. Church Membership Falls Below Majority for First Time," Gallup, March 29, 2021, https://news.gallup.com/poll/341963/church-membership-falls-below-majority-first-time.aspx.

3. "Modeling the Future of Religion in America," Pew Research Center, September 13, 2022, https://www.pewresearch.org/religion/2022/09/13/modeling-the-future-of-religion-in-america/.

4. Esther Larson, "Giving USA 2023: A Conversation About Faith and Giving," Philanthropy Roundtable, August 4, 2023, https://www.philanthropyroundtable.org/giving-usa-2023-a-conversation-about-faith-and-giving/.

5. Mark Chaves, *American Religion: Contemporary Trends*, 2nd ed. (Princeton University Press, 2017).

religiosity show just a little bit more erosion. The result, over time, is something of a crisis for institutional religion.

But the world isn't the same today as it was fifty years ago. In the same way that looking at video rentals in a streaming world won't give us an accurate picture of people's interest, looking at attendance or membership isn't likely to give us an accurate picture of religious interest in a disaffiliated world.

You read that correctly. We live in a disaffiliated *world*. I know the term "disaffiliated" is often used only to explain why those religious attendance numbers have declined so dramatically over the past few decades, but the church is not alone here. Look, for example, at voluntary associations and groups like Kiwanis, Rotary, Lions Club, and others. Membership and activity have declined to nearly a fraction of what they were at their height in the middle of the twentieth century.[6] The church is experiencing the same trend of disaffiliation that every other industry in the United States is facing.

In what is perhaps the most famous book in the social sciences to be written in the past fifty years, Robert Putnam addresses this phenomenon head-on. In 2000, he wrote *Bowling Alone: The Collapse and Revival of American Community* to document and address the loss of social connections that once made up the fabric of American society. What Putnam found in his investigation was an astonishing hollowing out of the kinds of organizational participation that were once defining features of American life.

> The church is experiencing the same trend of disaffiliation that every other industry in the United States is facing.

And I don't think anyone would argue that the 2000s have brought us closer together. If anything, we're more isolated and polarized than ever. It's as true for secular spaces as it is for religious

---

6. Robert D. Putnam, *Bowling Alone: The Collapse and Revival of American Community* (Simon & Schuster, 2000).

Trust
Confidence in Institutions

Institution	1970s	Today
Big Business	26%	23%
The Medical System	80%	36%
The Presidency	52%	38%
Television News	46%	18%
Congress	42%	11%
Newspapers	39%	23%
Public Schools	58%	29%
Banks	60%	30%
Organized Religion	65%	36%

Percent Answering "Great Deal / Quite a Lot" on a Five-Point Scale

Information from Lydia Saad, "Historically Low Faith in U.S. Institutions Continues," Gallup, July 6, 2023, https://news.gallup.com/poll/508169/historically-low-faith-institutions-continues.aspx.

spaces. In short, American life is moving away from institutions being the primary governing forces.

While it's not entirely clear what started this trend, we can pinpoint how it is expressed and felt in people's lives. Reputable research firms like Pew, Gallup, and the General Social Survey all point to a decline of trust in major social institutions as a defining feature of American life in the last fifty years. What they have collectively found is that as we have separated from one another, we've also become a lot less trusting.

Confidence in our bedrock social institutions, such as schools, the government, religion, business, and others, has been cut in half since the late 1970s, with most metrics at or near all-time lows in 2023.[7] Take a look at the decline of confidence in some of the most fundamental social institutions in the country over the last fifty years.

As discussed in chapter 1, this loss of trust is one of the enduring trends that is shaping our newest generations. Because their parents

---

7. Lydia Saad, "Historically Low Faith in U.S. Institutions Continues," Gallup, July 6, 2023, https://news.gallup.com/poll/508169/historically-low-faith-institutions-continues.aspx.

and those around them don't trust institutions, they don't participate in them unless they must. Institutional participation was once the default way of engaging in public life, but that's no longer the case.

However, just because we don't trust institutions and participate in them doesn't mean that we disregard those parts of our lives. We still find ways to be political and get an education and medical assistance even though we don't trust the political parties, schools, and insurance companies like we used to. As our trust in institutions has faded, we have created alternatives. The past few decades have seen the rise of homeschooling, homeopathic medicine, cryptocurrency, organic foods, and a whole range of innovations for meeting our basic needs without having to engage with traditional institutions.

Along the way, some of the old forms of those institutions have died out. For example, Blockbuster was replaced by Netflix and other streaming services. Nowhere is this more true than in the field of religion. The world has disaffiliated, but it hasn't stopped caring about God or life's biggest questions or sacred concerns.

In her fantastic 2013 book, *Sacred Stories, Spiritual Tribes: Finding Religion in Everyday Life*, Nancy Ammerman writes, "In a time of significant change, we cannot assume we will find religion in the predictable places or in the predictable forms. And if we do not find as much of it in those predictable places as we did before, we cannot assume that it is disappearing."[8] After this book came out, I had the privilege to hear Dr. Ammerman speak about the research, and she told me, "We are only just now coming to terms with the fact that more and more religion happens outside of traditional institutions."

I have never encountered something that resonated so deeply with what I was also seeing in my own life and research. We are indeed living in a time of significant change. Who could argue that? And as much as we find religion is practiced less in the "predictable" places, like pews and programmed small groups, we are, in fact, seeing more and more of it pop up in unpredictable places.

---

8. Nancy Tatom Ammerman, *Sacred Stories, Spiritual Tribes: Finding Religion in Everyday Life* (Oxford University Press, 2013), 6.

Just looking at the digital world, we can see that young people are exploring religion on TikTok and YouTube, following influencers and learning about everything from crystals, witchcraft, and manifestation to traditional institutional religions like Judaism and Christianity. There are massive communities on Discord linked to popular games like *Minecraft* and *Roblox* that host gatherings of people in religious services. Apps such as Headspace, Hallow, Insight Timer, Pray.com, and others are some of the most popular in the world and bring prayer and meditation right to people's mobile devices. Religiously themed podcasts are ubiquitous, from standard reproductions of sermons to increasingly popular podcasts that straddle the sacred and the secular, like *Harry Potter and the Sacred Text*, which not only has a thriving online community but hosts in-person gatherings and pilgrimages as well. We're even starting to see virtual reality religious and spiritual gatherings pop up as headsets like the Meta Quest and Apple's Vision Pro become more pervasive.

> To put it simply, the old metrics are the wrong numbers for a new era.

With all that in mind, it's clear that the problem with using the affiliation measurements of attendance, membership, and giving is not just that we incorrectly assess people's religiosity. The real problem is that it sends us in the wrong direction for action. As the old adage goes, "That which gets measured gets managed."

When we focus on membership, giving, and affiliation as the primary indicators of belief, we end up focusing our actions on those numbers. When we leap from a number to a conclusion without stopping to think about whether we've got the right number in the first place, we are in grave danger of spending a lot of time, energy, and other resources going in the wrong direction.

To put it simply, the old metrics are the wrong numbers for a new era, and our obsession with them is causing us to implement ineffective solutions for engaging young people in our ministries.

The old metrics have lost their utility because they are primarily markers of institutional connection, not personal religiosity. Think about it for just a second. Affiliation is about whether you're willing to align yourself and your identity with a religious institution, not about whether you believe in God. Attendance is about whether and how often you participate in the gatherings designated by the institution, not about how often you interact with the divine. Membership is about whether you're willing to make a long-term commitment to a local expression of the institutional church, not about whether you find yourself longing to participate in a community of people exploring the sacred. Financial tithing is about whether you want to use your money to support all the values espoused by the institution, not about whether your religious convictions surrounding charity and generosity are lived out in your everyday financial decisions.

For so long we have conflated these two sides of the coin, the institutional and the personal, because we used to live in a high-trust world. When people trusted institutions, these markers were pretty reliable indicators of a person's individual beliefs and identities. But as Nancy Ammerman cautions us, when the world changes, we shouldn't think our old metrics will still tell us what they once did. The reality is that we live in a disaffiliated world that doesn't trust institutions, and the metrics that rely on an assumption of trust aren't actually very useful anymore.

Hammers and Nails

I'm sure you've heard the old adage "When the only tool you have is a hammer, everything looks like a nail." I love this saying. I think about it a lot because it helps keep me honest and reminds me to check my biases and preconceived ideas. I often ask myself, Is this the best, right idea, or is it just the one I'm drawn to because I know it best?

This is the basic problem with continuing to focus on the old institutional measurements in this new low-trust world. We live in a low-trust world, but we keep trying to use tools developed for a high-trust society to fix our problems.

I think the flip side of that saying is also true: When all you can see are nails, the only tool you reach for is a hammer. I hit on this realization a few years ago when I was building an extension of the deck behind our house. My son was nine years old at the time, just old enough to be interested in what was happening but not really old enough to help much. To involve him and keep him safely out of the way of harm, I set him up with a small set of tools in the yard and some lumber scraps.

Not long into this setup I could hear his frustration, so I checked on him only to find that he was fervently hammering away . . . at a screw . . . with the back of a drill. He had tried banging on it with everything, he said, but it just wouldn't go in. He was so convinced that the screw was a nail that all he could see in the tools in front of him were various hammers.

Aside from the #ParentingFail, there's a real lesson embedded in there about using old metrics to try and understand faith and spirituality in the modern world. This incident serves as a metaphor for the ways in which traditional approaches to measuring religiosity and spiritual engagement may no longer fit contemporary experiences.

Just as using a hammer on a screw is ineffective, applying outdated metrics to modern spiritual practices can lead to misinterpretation and misguided strategies. If we want to genuinely understand and support today's diverse expressions of faith, we need to rethink our tools and methods. This recalibration is essential as we endeavor to guide a generation for whom faith may not be declining in importance but rather taking on new and varied forms that demand a different kind of acknowledgment and support.

High-Trust Tools

In a world that trusts institutions, the smart thing to do is to monitor attendance, affiliation, and giving. When those numbers decline, you should try to align yourself and your ministry as much as you can with the biggest, most important institution you can find so you can have as much influence as possible with the people in your community.

You lead with your title or the size of your congregation or how long your denomination has been around. You display your credentials conspicuously as evidence of your expertise, conveyed on you by as important a university as you could possibly get to let you in. These are our high-trust tools.

High-trust tools all have a critical component in common: the position that expertise and knowledge are in short supply. Nearly all our religious education, indeed most of our education systems in general, is built on the assumption that the expert has knowledge that needs to be transmitted to the student. The information contained by the expert is a scarce resource, and power flows to the person and institutions who can command that expertise.

In the religious world, this has historically meant that pastors, priests, directors of religious education, and other religious professionals are important gatekeepers. The institutions that certify these professionals have played an important credentialing role by signaling to the public that these people can be trusted. If you trust institutions, and the institution says it trusts this person, then the logic follows that you should trust this person.

When it comes to interacting with young people, you try to get them, literally, on your turf, in your building. The bigger and more stately, the better to convey confidence and certainty. You try to have the answers to all the questions. You have the best programs, the biggest gatherings, the coolest music. The teenager simply needs to show up.

These are excellent tools and approaches to engaging communities of young people in a high-trust world, and they have worked incredibly well for a long time. These high-trust tools were our hammers in a world full of nails.

High-Trust Tools in a Low-Trust World

In the low-trust world we live in now, the more you align yourself with an institution, the further you are set back. The more you lead with your expertise, credentials, certainty, and institutional size, the less influence you get in the life of a young person.

Information is no longer in short supply. In fact, it abounds. Your phone has more computing power than all NASA did in the 1960s.[9] Every day, we create 3.5 quintillion bytes of data. That's 3,500,000,000,000,000,000 pieces of information generated daily.[10] Anyone with access to the internet can learn whatever they want about any subject, including religion.

So when you come along and make the case that a young person has to listen to you to get answers to their questions or show up at your events or classes or programming to learn more about God or the divine, it simply doesn't hold water for them. It's out of step with the rest of their world.

> Anyone with access to the internet can learn whatever they want about any subject, including religion.

When you make attendance at an event (worship, lock-in, Bible study, etc.) on your church campus the precondition for engagement, the less success you're going to have. When you ask people to trust you not because you know them but because some other institution has conferred a title to you that certifies your expertise, you inspire *less* confidence.

This is not to say that the old tools and measures are bad. In fact, they worked remarkably well for generations. And they still sorta, kinda work right now. Trust in institutions has eroded, but it hasn't disappeared completely.

Youth directors often admit that despite their increasing efforts, the results seem to be waning year by year. These leaders are putting in more work than ever only to see diminishing returns for

---

9. Graham Kendall, "Your Mobile Phone vs. Apollo 11's Guidance Computer," RealClear Science, July 2, 2019, https://www.realclearscience.com/articles/2019/07/02/your_mobile_phone_vs_apollo_11s_guidance_computer_111026.html.

10. "Breaking Down Barriers to Data for All: Harnessing the Value of Data Democratization and Accessibility," Data Dynamics, accessed December 5, 2024, https://www.datadynamicsinc.com/blog-data-for-all-breaking-down-barriers-and-harnessing-the-value-of-data-democratization/.

their hard work over time. I hear this all the time from campus ministers, camp counselors, and youth directors. The following are direct quotes to me from youth ministry professionals just in the past couple of years:

> "I never thought it would be this hard just to get kids to show up."
>
> "Where are all the kids today? Like, I literally don't know where to find them if they're not at church."
>
> "I've been doing this for decades. You'd think I'd be better at it, but I'm working harder than I ever have. I have more experience and knowledge, but it just seems like I'm having less impact than when I started."

One of the great privileges and one of the great sadnesses of my life is hearing so many earnest and caring people express such profound frustration and helplessness.

What has become clear to me in these conversations is that the church is not dealing with a crisis of care. Religious professionals care enough. They're trying enough. They're working hard enough.

What we're dealing with is a lack of understanding.

We keep expecting high-trust tools to work in a low-trust world. And the reality is that they just don't work because they weren't designed that way. These tools weren't meant to get the screw to turn.

We need to develop new tools and metrics to reach young people in this new environment. This is the key challenge for our world today.

Low-Trust Tools

Thankfully, there's some really useful social science that can help us build and employ low-trust tools and measures to better match our disaffiliated world. The key to all these tools is a refocus on relationships.¹¹ But not just any kind of relationships. Relationships that are effective at building real trust among people contain particular elements and need to be tracked and implemented systematically.

In 2015, when I was a university professor, I started working on a concept that I called relational authority to capture the best way to influence and lead people in the age of low trust and disaffiliation. At first I applied it in voluntary groups and associations, but then I moved the concept over to the religious world because I kept seeing applications there in my research. The concept explained so much that I actually made it the focus of our inaugural *State of Religion and Young People* report at Springtide Research Institute, where I led a team of researchers to figure out how relational authority could be applied to help trusted adults influence the lives of young people.[12]

The basic premise of relational authority is that we live in a world where expertise is not enough if we really want to influence others. In fact, if we show up only as the expert in someone's life, they tend to tune us out pretty quickly.

I first noticed this with my students. Since I was their professor and in charge of their grades, I could get compliance. But they wouldn't actually trust that I had their best interests in mind or let me have any real influence over them just because I had a PhD and a title. It wasn't until I sat with them in my office, expressed real interest in their lives, shared things about my own life, took notes, and followed up that I started to crack through the shell. Although I came to accept this as fact, I didn't understand the why behind it at first.

I was the same person in front of the classroom that I was in my office. Often I was saying more or less the same things—nothing

---

11. Josh Packard and Megan Bissell, "Research Backed Practices to Engage Youth in a Vibrant Catholic Church: The Case for Implementing Sacred Listening Practices," *Journal of Moral Theology* 13, special issue no. 2 (2024): 252–70, https://jmt.scholasticahq.com/article/125234-research-based-practices-to-engage-youth-in-a-vibrant-catholic-church-the-case-for-implementing-sacred-listening-practices.

12. Springtide Research Institute, *The State of Religion and Young People 2020: Relational Authority* (Springtide Research Institute, 2020).

revolutionary, by the way. I was saying the things professors have always said to students: "If you apply yourself, you could do really well in my class." "You are more capable than you might think you are." "If you do the reading, I think you'll find a lot more application for that theory." "You should really try to drink less and study more." And so on and so forth.

It wasn't until years later, when I was doing the research at Springtide, that a former student made it clear for me. She said, "When you were just a professor in the classroom, I assumed that you had the university's best interests in mind, or maybe your own. Your degree, your expertise, your title. They all came from these fancy institutions that don't care about me. But in your office, you got to know me, and I saw that you were actually trying to use all of that to help *me*."

The authority that I was working with in front of the classroom actually pointed back to an institution that my students didn't trust. I thought I was conveying certainty and building their confidence in me as an expert they could trust. But I was actually moving backward in that regard.

At Springtide Research Institute, we broke down relational authority into its various elements. By then I knew that expertise was necessary, but not enough, to get influence. After all, those students weren't sitting in the office with just anybody. My position, credentials, and title mattered a little bit, and it would have been a bigger issue if I claimed to be an expert in a university setting without a PhD or title or role that conveyed some authority. But those things weren't enough.

The research uncovered four other elements that, when used along with expertise, can help rebuild trust. Listening, integrity, transparency, and care are the essential elements for gaining trust and influence in someone's life.

What is interesting about those four additional elements is that by themselves, they aren't enough either. If all you do is show up and listen, demonstrate integrity, be transparent, and care, young people will almost certainly *like* you, but you won't break into the realm of actual influence. You also need to bring some insight, perspective, experience, or information to the table that makes you an expert. The magic is in the combination of these elements, not in the abandonment of expertise.

Expertise Is Necessary, but It's Not Sufficient

So let's look at each of those elements. We know what expertise is, but what about the other four: listening, integrity, transparency, and care?

Listening

Listening is probably the single most important thing an adult can do to gain trust with a young person. Young people tell us over and over again that they feel dismissed, invisible, or even unseen by the adults in their lives. Asking questions and expressing genuine interest is disarming in that context. It flips the script on what they expect from you. Using phrases like "Tell me more about that" and "Can you explain _____ to me?" (where the blank is something you know they're passionate or knowledgeable about), can go a long ways toward establishing trust.

The problem for a lot of adults is that they don't have to listen to a young person for very long to hear some truly alarming things. Whether it's a song they like, thoughts about religion and faith, a relationship they're in, or a career decision, young people who are trying to make sense of the world say and do things that can make us concerned for them very quickly. And we think if we just listen without correcting them, then the young person we're talking to will see our silence as tacit approval.

So we're constantly tempted to step in and be the expert and at least voice our disapproval or express judgment in some way. We feel the need to correct. But remember, young people live in judgment all day, every day. They expect adults to judge everything they do. What they often want and need, though, is an adult who will listen first. There will be time for correction and judgment later, but if you rush into it, if you can't just listen to understand and empathize, then you're back to leading with your expertise. You're telling that young person, essentially, "I know what's best for you. You don't know. You're too young/immature/inexperienced." It's an approach that works in a high-trust world but has almost no utility in a low-trust environment.

In our own survey of American teenagers about the importance of listening, *Sacred Listening, Deeper Faith*, young people were very clear about what made them feel heard and what did not.[13] When asked for the top three aspects of listening that were critical for building trust, they listed attentiveness, empathy, and nonjudgmental responses. Listening without expressing judgment also leads to increased feelings of connection and actually deepens the young person's faith. Perhaps most importantly, it keeps the lines of communication open. When asked about the biggest barriers to effective listening in their faith communities or personal relationships, the number one answer was, "I fear being judged for my opinions or beliefs."

This idea of listening to understand brings us to an essential psychological principle: unconditional positive regard. Developed by Carl Rogers, this concept is about accepting and valuing someone for who they are without any conditions or judgments.[14] In the context of conversing with young people, it means creating a space where they feel not just heard but genuinely accepted—even when they share views or make decisions that we find concerning or alarming.

The beauty of unconditional positive regard is that it allows for an open dialogue without the looming threat of judgment. It gives young people the freedom to explore their thoughts and feelings, offering them a safe emotional space, which is so often missing in their lives. Educator Alex Venet notes that this has become a centrally important practice in her classroom. Essentially, she writes, the core message is "I care about you. You have value. You

---

13. Future of Faith, *Sacred Listening, Deeper Faith: A Research-Driven Approach* (Future of Faith, 2025), https://www.futureoffaith.org/sacredlisteningstudy.

14. C. R. Rogers, "The Necessary and Sufficient Conditions of Therapeutic Personality Change," *Journal of Consulting Psychology* 21, no. 2 (1957): 95–103, https://doi.org/10.1037/h0045357.

don't have to do anything to prove it to me, and nothing's going to change my mind."[15]

As much as you might already know this to be true about the young people in your life, it's very likely that the young people don't know you feel that way. Genuine listening that seeks to understand, not to correct, can help bridge that gap and convey how much you care in a way that young people will be receptive to.

Integrity

Integrity, for young people, is simple. It means doing what you say you will do. If, for some reason, you can't make good on your word, then apologize and admit you were wrong. Young people love to see adults admit when they're wrong, not because they want to see adults knocked down a peg (OK, maybe it's some of that) but because they *know* adults in their lives aren't perfect. They're fine with that. But they can't handle adults pretending to be right all the time. They see it as dishonest. So if you're wrong or you don't know or life gets in the way of a commitment, own your mistake. Communicate your intention, explain the situation, apologize, and ask for forgiveness.

Transparency

Transparency is tricky. Young people really want to know about your life, especially to the extent that your experiences overlap with their own. But we have to be careful about sharing things in age-appropriate ways. Your experience getting caught shoplifting as a teenager might have some important lessons about peer pressure, honesty, and consequences to teach a young person, but it probably needs to be shared differently with a twelve-year-old than with an eighteen-year-old—or maybe not.

A friend of mine works with at-risk youth who have done and seen things at very young ages that I wasn't even aware of until

---

15. Alex Shevrin Venet, "How Unconditional Positive Regard Can Help Students Feel Cared For," *MindShift*, KQED, May 25, 2021, https://www.kqed.org/mindshift/57646/how-unconditional-positive-regard-can-help-students-feel-cared-for.

much later in life. Those kids need some real proof that you understand them. Drugs, family trauma, and violence are all too often a part of their lives. My friend can't treat them like my youth leaders treated me at thirteen years old; they would laugh her out of the room.

Only you, the expert in the life of the young person across from you, can know what the right things are to share. Knowing what's right comes from listening first. But make no mistake, sharing things from your own life is critically important.

When you talk about the doubts you have, the mistakes you've made, and the people who helped you along the way, you're slowly dissolving the boundary between you and that young person. You're becoming part of the reference group of the young person in front of you.

Care

Finally, we come to care. Young people experience care from adults in a very specific way. It basically comes down to time and attention. They know that time, not money or anything else, is the scarcest commodity for adults.

Care is expressed by taking time to intentionally reach out to them and be in the same physical or digital locations. It can be a text in the middle of the day just to say that you're thinking about them. It can mean showing up to their school play, writing them a note in the actual mail, or dropping into their *Minecraft* server to help them build for a while. Really, it's just anything that shows you are intentionally thinking about them.

Relational Authority in the Wild

Those five things are incredibly powerful and become the gateway to being a trusted expert in a young person's life. In fact, if you think back to the adults you trusted, or peers you trust currently, I'd be willing to bet that they exhibited many of those traits without even thinking about it.

It's important to understand that you probably are already naturally doing some of these five things—listening, integrity, transparency, care, and expertise—and that it's impossible to try and do all of them at once. Give yourself some grace, but keep the larger point in mind. Don't lead only with expertise; those days are over. And don't just try to be their friend and only do the first four. If you put all your focus there, they won't really respect your insights.

If you can find some balance between the five, you'll gain their trust, enabling you to be one of the adults that young people turn to when they have questions or a decision to make. You'll have the trust you need to step in when you see a potential pitfall coming or trouble on the horizon. In short, you'll get to do the work with them that drew you into your role in the first place.

None of this should come as a surprise. In fact, other industries have sort of stumbled into this same relational authority model. If we look at how marketers are approaching this generation, we will see time and again a focus on decentralizing the authoritative voice, privileging community and relationships, and listening to consumers. These organizations are not interested in influencing young people in the same way you are, but they are certainly trying to capture young people's attention and purchasing decisions, and they're leveraging some of the key factors of relational authority to do it. In each of these examples, you'll find that traditional expertise is lurking in there, but it's not the only voice, and it's never decoupled from relationships.[16]

Apple. Apple's "Shot on iPhone" campaign features user-generated content from iPhone users around the world. The campaign highlights the quality of the iPhone camera and showcases the creativity and diversity of the Apple community.

---

16. For more about company reputation, see "Most Trusted Brands 2021," Morning Consult, accessed December 5, 2024, https://morningconsult.com/most-trusted-brands-2021/; Kantar, "BrandZ Top 100 Most Valuable Global Brands 2020," SyncForce, accessed December 5, 2024, https://www.rankingthebrands.com/The-Brand-Rankings.aspx?rankingID=6&year=1334; and "The 2020 Axios Harris Poll 100 Reputation Rankings," Axios, July 30, 2020, https://www.axios.com/2020/07/30/axios-harris-poll-corporate-reputations-2020.

Adidas. Adidas's "Here to Create" campaign features athletes, musicians, and other creatives who are breaking down barriers and creating something new. The campaign emphasizes the idea that everyone has the power to create and that Adidas is there to support and empower them in their journey.

Burger King. Burger King's "The Moldy Whopper" campaign aims to promote the company's removing artificial preservatives from its burgers. The ad features time-lapse footage of a Whopper decaying over time, highlighting the natural ingredients in the burger and the company's commitment to transparency.

Glossier. Glossier is a beauty brand that has become extremely popular with Gen Z due to its focus on relationships and community building. The brand often features real customers in its ad campaigns and encourages its followers to share their own makeup looks and beauty tips on social media.

Nike. Nike's "You Can't Stop Us" campaign was a huge hit with younger generations due to its emphasis on inclusivity and diversity. The ad features athletes of all backgrounds and abilities, highlighting the idea that anyone can achieve greatness with hard work and determination.

Lululemon. Lululemon's focus on total wellness has captured young people as they move away from one-size-fits-all models of health. Lululemon's annual *Global Wellbeing Report* focuses on all aspects of health and well-being for diverse groups of people.

It should come as no surprise, then, that the brands above consistently rank among the most trusted for Gen Z. I don't think the church world should normally be looking to for-profit companies for guidance, but these are not normal times, and these companies have figured out how to garner trust with young people at a time when the church is losing it. It's worth seeing how they use the principles of relational authority to become trusted in the eyes of young people. We need to find a new pathway to trust in a world where institutional authority alone isn't seen as trustworthy, and these brands have figured it out.

The model of relational authority presented above helps uncover and build those pathways in systematic ways in ministry as well. When I was at Springtide Research Institute, we tested this model of relational authority with young people and evaluated it explicitly for measures of trust. What we found was that while trust in institutions and institutional authority is low and declining, trust in the elements of relational authority are in the ninetieth percentile for young people.[17]

You've probably seen ministries that have figured this out as well. One example that is worth exploring more comes from Jason Lief and Kurt Rietema. In their 2023 book *To Mend the World: A New Vision for Youth Ministry*, they describe how social entrepreneurship offered up a way to be in relationship with the young people in their neighborhood. In their examples, you can see the principles of relational authority at work naturally, and the outcomes for the young people, the neighborhood, and the church are outstanding. They describe showing up in the lives of young people as part expert and part caring adult. While the thing they're working on certainly matters, the larger project is the kids themselves. I'm willing to bet that you've naturally seen traction in the parts of your own ministry that leverage these elements, even if you weren't designing explicitly for them.

Relational Metrics

All of this is only part of the equation to build trust with young people, though. I'm very aware that if we're going to shift focus to relationships over programs, we're going to need new metrics. We need to get religious leaders and supervisors to understand how to truly measure what matters when it comes to engaging young people today and why those metrics are so vital for a church to flourish for decades to come.

I opened this chapter by noting that movie rentals are not a good way to assess our collective interests in movies anymore. Streaming numbers and clicks need to be added to the equation with ticket sales at real theaters.

17. Springtide Research Institute, *State of Religion and Young People 2020*.

So what's the ministry equivalent? What relational metrics need to be added alongside the traditional numbers of attendance, baptisms, confirmations, and so on?

In their 2023 article in *The Atlantic* titled "American Religion Is Not Dead Yet" authors Wendy Cadge and Elan Babchuck point us in the right direction. They write, "The old metrics of success—attendance and affiliation, or, more colloquially, 'butts, budgets, and buildings'—may no longer capture the state of American religion. Although participation in traditional religious settings (churches, synagogues, mosques, schools, etc.) is in decline, signs of life are popping up elsewhere: in conversations with chaplains, in communities started online that end up forming in-person bonds as well, in social-justice groups rooted in shared faith." So rather than asking how many people went to church last Sunday morning, Cadge and Babchuck suggest that we ask, "Where are Americans finding meaning in their lives? How are they marking the passing of sacred time? Where are they building pockets of vibrant communities? And what are they doing to answer the prophetic call, however it is that they hear it? There have never been more ways to answer these questions, even if fewer and fewer people are stepping into a sanctuary."[18]

I think their assessment is exactly right. The goal of religion isn't (just) to get people to come to church on Sunday morning in a building and give their money. Religious leaders are also interested in soul transformation, meaning making, and encounters with the sacred.

If we really believe what the research tells us, that young people experience the sacred and transformative primarily through relationships, then we need to start tracking their relationships. Instead of wondering how many people showed up, we need to start asking different questions, like, *How many points of contact did you have this week? What was the nature of those interactions?*

---

18. Wendy Cadge and Elan Babchuck, "American Religion Is Not Dead Yet," *Atlantic*, January 16, 2023, https://www.theatlantic.com/politics/archive/2023/01/us-religious-affiliation-rates-declining/672729/.

Are they moving to include conversations more frequently about values and beliefs and the divine? Was prayer involved? Who initiated the contact? and other similar data points.

All these daily things that make up a transformational and trusted relationship can be tracked systematically on a simple spreadsheet in a way similar to how we track attendance, affiliation, and giving. With the collaborative power of Google Sheets or Excel, the data can even be shared with staff and volunteers.

While the magic of *what* to say to a young person will always rely on thoughtful, well-trained adults, you can build a system to make sure that each young person in your community is being supported by you or someone on your team as you support those who support young people.

Let me share with you one real-world example of this that I know well. I'm good friends with Jeff Neel, the executive director of Northern Colorado Youth for Christ, our local Youth for Christ chapter. A few years ago, Jeff realized that though what he and the team were doing with young people was all centered on relationships, as their organization grew, they were starting to lose track of the details of the interactions with the hundreds of kids who were showing up every week. Additionally, they needed some way to know that when leaders were spending time with a young person, they weren't just hanging out with them.

So he built an app to track every interaction between a young person and his staff. With just a few clicks after each meaningful interaction, the staff member can update the app with the nature of the encounter and other important details so that everyone else on the team has access to it too. This ensures some continuity of knowledge across the entire team.

Perhaps more importantly, it allows them to map these interactions onto a theory of faith development that includes very deliberate relational and spiritual milestones. The power of this framework is that it allows for hanging out with a young person to be intentional. When implemented correctly, it means that each interaction and conversation can take on a more directed purpose than *only* hanging out. They are able to systematically move young people from one stage to the next over a period of time.

Of course, that movement is not quick, and it doesn't happen linearly. There are times that they have to go back nearly to square one. But they always know where they are and where they're headed.

You and your organization might have different values or stages of development that you want to track, but you can see the power of a system like this. This approach helps direct and scale relationships beyond the carrying capacity of any one individual.

It also helps communicate in tangible, concrete ways the impact they're making on a weekly, quarterly, and annual basis, which is important for everything from internal feedback and reviews to communicating with donors, foundations, board members, and other stakeholders.[19]

By finding a way to measure the things Cadge and Babchuck mention above, the leaders of Northern Colorado Youth for Christ are not only making the case for funding and support from the community, but they're actively able to focus on the things that truly matter in the faith lives of young people.

Over the years, this approach has led to hundreds of baptisms and a thriving ministry site that also checks all the traditional boxes of attendance numbers and financial health. In other words, if you can measure, track, and invest in relational low-trust tools, then you're going to find that your institution is strengthened as well.

---

19. If you want to know more about this approach, feel free to contact Jeff directly at Jeff@ncyfc.org.

MAPPING TRUSTED RELATIONSHIPS:
A Step-by-Step Guide

Introduction

In today's low-trust environment, it is crucial for youth workers to grasp the relational dynamics affecting young individuals, particularly in faith discussions. Connection arises from relational authority, where expertise melds with listening, integrity, transparency, and care. This harmonious blend will allow you to engage in conversations that are not just informed but also deeply meaningful and safe.

It is vital to understand a young person's circle of influence, which can include family, friends, mentors, digital influencers, and others. This will reveal insights into their faith perspectives, confidants, and openness to discussion.

The essential first step to this understanding is deep, empathetic listening—an active process of connecting beyond words. A good listener is a trusted figure who learns from the positive examples in a young person's life.

The activity below guides young people in mapping their trust networks. This will help you comprehend relational dynamics and allow young people to articulate their trust networks, shedding light on the role of faith in their relationships. Rooted in the meaningful work of

SACRED LISTENING TOOL

Dave Rahn from Arbor Research, this activity will give you a window into the hearts and lives of the young people you serve.

Objectives

- Help youth ministers gauge the social and spiritual landscapes of their young members by mapping out key relationships and faith interactions.
- Encourage self-reflection and open dialogue among young people about their relationships and spiritual lives, fostering a deeper sense of community.
- Use gathered insights to empower youth ministers to craft more relevant and impactful programming, discussions, and support structures.
- Broaden the impact of this activity beyond the youth demographic, fostering stronger, more interconnected faith communities.

Pre-Activity Preparation

Materials Needed

- Notecards (one for each participant)
- Colored markers or pens
- Whiteboard or poster board
- Dry-erase markers (if using a whiteboard)

Step 1: Set the Intention (*Imago Dei*)

Begin by establishing the sacredness of each person and the relationships they share. Frame the exercise as an opportunity to see these connections as reflections of the divine. This phase sets the tone, emphasizing the importance of understanding relationships not just as social ties but as sacred connections that can deepen one's spiritual journey.

As we dive into the core part of this exercise, we're getting ready to explore the terrain of relationships and spirituality through some simple shapes and words. But don't let the simplicity fool you; these circles, squares, and triangles are going to tell us a lot about who's central in the lives of your young people and why. The young people will draw shapes to represent the people they engage with daily, trust deeply, and talk to about their faith. A few additional markers and text will provide context about their spiritual habits and wishes. This isn't just doodling; it's an introspective journey mapped out on a notecard. By the end of it, you'll have a miniblueprint of their social and spiritual worlds, which you can later dissect, discuss, and find meaningful paths to enrich.

Open with something like, "Today, we're going to explore the relationships that matter most to you—the people you trust and who influence your life. These relationships are sacred because they help shape who you are."

Optionally, include a brief ritual, such as a moment of silence or a shared reading, to create a reflective atmosphere.

Step 2: Ask and Record (Alignment)

Participants each receive a notecard and a marker. They will use simple shapes to represent different types of relationships on the front of the card. Follow these prompts:

- Circle: Draw a circle for every person you talk to most days. Put the person's initials inside the circle.
- Square: Draw a square for each person you trust with your secrets. If someone is already a circle, put the square around the circle. Put their initials inside the shape if you haven't already done so.
- Triangle: Draw a triangle for every person you talk to about your faith life. The same rules apply—surround existing shapes if needed. Put their initials inside the shape if you haven't already done so.

Next, direct the participants to do some simple counting and recording.

- Bottom right corner: Write the number of the people on the notecard who are in your immediate family.
- Bottom left corner: Write the number of times you go to church or another religious service per month.
- Top right corner: Write how many times per week you have conversations about faith.
- Top left corner: Write an X if you wish you had more conversations about faith.
- Back: Finally, flip the card. On the back, write down a conversation topic you might like to have about faith or a type of discussion you'd like to have with an adult about faith. Place your own initials in the bottom right corner.

Throughout the exercise, pause to engage in group conversations about any questions that arise, including definitional questions, such as, Does _____ count as a secret? What does it mean to "talk" to someone in a day? What counts as "talking"? These conversations are great opportunities for formation.

Step 3: Share and Reflect (Pattern Recognition)

Once the maps are completed, participants should gather to reflect on their maps. The focus here should be on recognizing patterns in their relationships, such as whom they talk to most, whom they trust, and how much overlap exists between these groups. This reflection will allow them to consider how faith fits into their trusted relationships.

Facilitate discussion by asking,

- Were you surprised by how few or how many people you have in certain categories?
- What did you notice about the overlap between whom you trust and whom you talk to about faith?
- How can these insights help you grow in your relationships and faith life?

Allow participants to journal their reflections if they prefer, encouraging them to think about what they learned from mapping their relationships.

Encourage everyone to share one thing they learned or felt. Tell them you'll use their questions as guideposts for future activities and discussions.

Step 4: Extending Relationships (Scaling Up, Out, and Down)

This follow-up phase ensures that the exercise's insights will contribute to scaling relationships in three dimensions—up, out, and down.

- Scaling up: Collect all the notecards and enter the data into a tracking sheet. This will allow for patterns in trusted relationships and faith conversations to inform future programming or group discussions. Use these insights to plan content that will resonate with the group's relational and spiritual needs.
- Scaling out: Encourage participants to use what they've learned to connect with new people in the community. Facilitate discussions between youth and adult congregants who share similar faith questions or concerns, broadening the scope of relational ministry.
- Scaling down: Identify participants who marked an X on their cards (indicating they wish for more faith conversations). Follow up personally with these individuals to offer one-on-one or small-group opportunities for deeper faith discussions, helping to nurture those relationships more intentionally.

Conclusion

This activity is more than just youth centered; it's about understanding the dynamics of relationships within your faith community. The intention here is to build a stronger, more integrated network of trusted relationships that will not just nurture individual faith but fortify the community.

4

BELONGING PRECEDES BELIEVING

The Loneliest Generation

When you think of Gen Z and Gen Alpha, what are the first words that come to mind? I think of terms like "technology," "connected," "social media," "activist," and "justice." Some word clouds from popular search engines feature terms such as "diverse," "digital native," and "global." If you work directly with young people, you might also think of some of their struggles. I've heard people use terms like "COVID generation," "mental health," and "disaffiliated."

But almost nobody comes up with the single biggest issue facing young people today: loneliness.

Gen Z is the loneliest generation ever.

That's an astonishing fact confirmed first by a massive study from Cigna of over twenty thousand Americans in 2018 and subsequently by a number of researchers.[1] You might wonder how it's possible to establish which generation is the loneliest. All reputable

---

1. "Cigna 2018 U.S. Loneliness Index," Cigna, May 2018, https://legacy.cigna.com/assets/docs/newsroom/loneliness-survey-2018-updated-fact-sheet.pdf.

studies in this area use a standard scale developed by researchers at UCLA in the late 1970s. The instrument has been validated and has been used hundreds of times in the last forty-five years, making it one of the more robust measures in social science.

Cigna's study was completed well before the pandemic, and it's safe to say that the effects of COVID-19 have only served to increase loneliness and isolation, especially among young people.

If loneliness is so rampant among young people, why isn't it the *first* thing we think about when we think about young people?

I think it's because it's so counterintuitive to do so.

Let me try an exercise slightly different from the one that opened this chapter. Instead of thinking of the words that come to mind when you think of Gen Z or Gen Alpha, think of the first image that you picture.

I bet I can guess what's in your picture. If you do a quick Google image search or look through any stock photo site for pictures of Gen Z or even just "young people," you'll find countless images of teenagers looking at their phones. Some of them will be happy, some will be sad, some will be alone, some together. But almost invariably, they will be on a device.

How can a generation be simultaneously connected to the entire world all the time and experiencing record levels of loneliness? It just doesn't make sense.

And yet we all know it's true. We know from our own experiences with our children and the young people we work with that loneliness and isolation are their reality. We know from surveys conducted by companies like Cigna and the office of the US Surgeon General, and we hear it from academics and other researchers in interviews and conversations with young people.

The Epidemic of Loneliness

The consequences of this situation are heartbreaking but not at all surprising. Loneliness is a condition that colors all aspects of health. Researchers have found implications for physical, social, and emotional health.

Dr. Julianne Holt-Lunstad is a renowned researcher in the field of social psychology. Her groundbreaking research has unveiled a sobering truth: Loneliness, often seen as an emotional state, can have severe physical consequences. One of her seminal studies drew a startling parallel, equating the health risks of chronic loneliness to that of smoking up to fifteen cigarettes daily.[2] This revelation underscores the tangible toll of social isolation on our well-being. Loneliness is also associated with an increased risk of cardiovascular issues, weakened immune function, and even cognitive decline. It's a reminder that our social connections, or the lack thereof, can profoundly affect our physical health, making it imperative to prioritize fostering meaningful connections in our lives.

Loneliness in teenagers is also associated with a range of other physical health problems, including poor sleep, increased inflammation, and increased stress. Additionally, loneliness has been linked to a range of emotional problems in young people, including depression, anxiety, and suicidal thoughts. It can also make it harder for teenagers to regulate their emotions and cope with stress.

All this led Dr. Vivek Murthy, the US surgeon general, to issue an advisory in 2023 titled "Our Epidemic of Loneliness and Isolation," which points to loneliness as one of the most challenging and important issues of our time: "Loneliness is far more than just a bad feeling—it harms both individual and societal health. It is associated with a greater risk of cardiovascular disease, dementia, stroke, depression, anxiety, and premature death. . . . And the harmful consequences of a society that lacks social connection can be felt in our schools, workplaces, and civic organizations, where performance, productivity, and engagement are diminished."[3] In

---

2. Julianne Holt-Lunstad, Timothy B. Smith, and J. Bradley Layton, "Social Relationships and Mortality Risk: A Meta-Analytic Review," *PLOS Medicine* 7, no. 7 (2010), https://doi.org/10.1371/journal.pmed.1000316.

3. Vivek H. Murthy, *Our Epidemic of Loneliness and Isolation: The U.S. Surgeon General's Advisory on the Healing Effects of Social Connection and Community* (US Department of Health and Human Services, 2023), 4.

other words, researchers and leaders from across different fields recognize a crisis of loneliness that is affecting all areas of society. The pandemic that we all just lived through exacerbated this significantly. Fewer Americans now than ever count themselves as having three or more close friends.

Over time, this loss of connection becomes self-reinforcing. The more we live without strong networks and good social lives, the more we actually forget even *how* to create and maintain these fundamental relationships. The longer we operate at a deficit of relationships, the harder it gets to find our way back.

The Experience of Loneliness for Young People

When we experience loneliness and isolation, the result is more profound than simple unhappiness. Prolonged periods of loneliness can actually lead to alterations in the brain's structure and function. Neurologically, the brain's stress response system becomes hyperactive, resulting in the release of stress hormones like cortisol. This chronic activation can lead to neural changes, particularly in regions associated with emotional regulation and social processing.

Loneliness is also linked to increased activity in brain areas associated with self-referential thinking, fostering a heightened self-focus that perpetuates feelings of isolation. In a recent article in *The Atlantic* titled "How America Got Mean," David Brooks addresses this as one of the root sources of our collective lack of civility:

> Expecting people to build a satisfying moral and spiritual life on their own by looking within themselves is asking too much. A culture that leaves people morally naked and alone leaves them without the skills to be decent to one another. Social trust falls partly because more people are untrustworthy. That creates crowds of what psychologists call "vulnerable narcissists." We all know grandiose narcissists—people who revere themselves as the center of the universe. Vulnerable narcissists are the more common figures

in our day—people who are also addicted to thinking about themselves, but who often feel anxious, insecure, avoidant. Intensely sensitive to rejection, they scan for hints of disrespect. Their self-esteem is wildly in flux. Their uncertainty about their inner worth triggers cycles of distrust, shame, and hostility.[4]

We can probably all identify strands of vulnerable narcissism among the young people that we work with—for example, an intense impulse to retreat from public life to avoid even the possibility of ridicule while simultaneously craving public affirmation. Maybe our first impulse in these situations is to tell young people to suck it up and get back out there. (Or maybe I'm just channeling my high school football coach.) Challenges are a part of growing up, we want to say, but it's not a reason to disengage with society altogether.

I think there's some truth in that. But loneliness is a little different from most of the typical teenage problems. Earlier in this chapter I noted that Cigna's research found young people to be the loneliest of any generation in their study. Perhaps even more importantly, it was the first time this had ever happened. Whenever the loneliness scale has been used in the past, it has always been the oldest generations that score the highest. The reasons are pretty obvious if you stop to think about it. We lose connections later in life as we tend to stop working, mobility is limited, and friends, family, and acquaintances sometimes move or pass away.

But we don't really know how to respond to profound loneliness among teenagers. It would seem that they should be the most socially connected. Most of them are surrounded by their peers all day at school and work. Many of them have tremendous amounts of discretionary time to spend doing things they love with other people, such as sports or participating in the arts, and

---

4. David Brooks, "How America Got Mean: In a Culture Devoid of Moral Education, Generations Are Growing Up in a Morally Inarticulate, Self-Referential World," *Atlantic*, August 14, 2023, https://www.theatlantic.com/magazine/archive/2023/09/us-culture-moral-education-formation/674765/.

as mentioned above, the internet affords them opportunities to connect with people like them all over the world.

Nevertheless, the facts remain. In study after study, we see that young people are simply lonely and increasingly isolated from one another and the rest of the world. For clues to how we should respond to this, I think we need to look a bit further into how this disconnection is actually experienced.

When you get excluded or left out of a group, or even when you perceive that you're being left out, your brain does some interesting things. The feeling of forced loneliness gets processed in the same part of your brain that processes physical pain and produces a similar release of cortisol.[5] You might remember from your science classes that cortisol is sometimes referred to as the "stress hormone" because it helps us deal with acute pain. But prolonged, elevated amounts of cortisol can have very negative effects, including mood disturbances.[6]

It is critical to understand that the regions of the brain that process social pain are the same ones that process physical pain. In a sense, when you're experiencing loneliness or isolation, you experience a pain response similar to the one you would experience if somebody dropped a hammer on your foot. Add in the already volatile chemistry of the average teenager, and you've got a recipe for disaster if there's no intervention.

The implications of this change everything about how we should interact with young people. My wife, like many of you, is a mandatory reporter. If she has good knowledge and reason to believe that a child is in physical danger, she is required to alert the proper authorities. I'm guessing that none of us would hesitate to step in and protect a child in physical danger. But if the brain processes social pain in the same way that it processes physical

---

5. Naomi I. Eisenberger, Matthew D. Lieberman, and Kipling D. Williams, "Does Rejection Hurt? An fMRI Study of Social Exclusion," *Science* 302, no. 5643 (2003): 290–92, https://doi.org/10.1126/science.1089134.

6. S. S. Dickerson and M. E. Kemeny, "Acute Stressors and Cortisol Responses: A Theoretical Integration and Synthesis of Laboratory Research," *Psychological Bulletin* 130, no. 3 (2004): 355–91, https://doi.org/10.1037/0033-2909.130.3.355.

pain, perhaps we should start expanding our definition of what counts as an emergency and needs our response. We might even need to rethink what needs mandatory reporting and the immediate attention of caring adults.

The Challenge for Caring Adults

When we think about who we are and how we came to be, one of the questions in the back of our mind should always be why. Why are we this way? Why have we evolved to this point? What's the utility of experiencing social exclusion as a form of pain? For the evolutionary biologists and others who study these kinds of things, these questions take them back to an even more fundamental question: Why do we have any pain at all? When you hold your finger close to a fire or accidentally touch a hot pan, you get an immediate pain response. In some ways, you might think that the agony associated with the burn is irritating, but it's actually a safety issue. The pain response tells you, "Stop doing this right now. Pull your hand away from this really hot pan before you do some lasting damage."

That's largely what is going on with the feeling of pain from social exclusion as well. We are such social creatures that we need a dramatic and instant sort of pain response from being excluded to remind us that isolation is not sustainable. It's like our body saying, "We can't go on like this for long. You're about to really hurt yourself if you keep going down this path." The pain of loneliness is, in some ways, your body telling you that you need to change your behavior and return to the group.

The sense of pain that we feel being left out of a group is actually a protective mechanism. It's intended to guide us back toward social, sustainable interactions and relationships with people. For a long period of time, maybe up until this exact point in history, that's about all we needed. It was not physically possible in many ways to stay excluded from the group. Leaving the tribe meant, in many cases, that we would actually die.

What's so weird about the time we live in, though, is that people can now choose the other route. In the midst of the pain that we feel from social exclusion, we can choose to exclude ourselves further. We can actually live alone, or at least apart, even though we are not designed or intended to.

What sociologists have been uncovering in recent years is an intense form of retreatism, which we call "network closure," as a response and contributor to isolation and loneliness. People build up walls, only letting in others that they already know and trust deeply. Instead of the pain response compelling them to change their behaviors to become more communal, they're closing ranks and becoming more individualistic because the technology and conveniences of modern life make it possible for the first time.

Unfortunately, the response that keeps us from the immediate pain of exclusion further contributes to our long-term loneliness. It's a lifestyle of stranger danger, which might be really useful for five-year-olds but doesn't work so well when you're a young adult trying to live a thriving, flourishing life.

Loneliness and Spiritual Health

While all this is concerning to anyone who cares about young people, you might be thinking that it falls outside your particular lane. After all, while you certainly care about the whole health of young people and want to see them thrive, you can't fix everything, and your primary concern is their faith and spiritual lives.

But the consequences for their spiritual health are just as severe. Loneliness and isolation have profound implications for a person's ability to engage with their spirituality or participate in religious practices. Individuals experiencing chronic loneliness often struggle to find solace or meaning in their spiritual or religious beliefs due to a sense of disconnection.[7]

Loneliness can also erode self-worth and purpose, creating barriers to connecting with one's spirituality. The real or perceived lack

---

7. John T. Cacioppo and William Patrick, *Loneliness: Human Nature and the Need for Social Connection* (Norton, 2008).

of support from a religious community can even intensify feelings of detachment and hinder engagement with faith-based practices.

Furthermore, loneliness can foster skepticism and doubt toward spiritual beliefs. When individuals feel abandoned and disconnected, they may question the existence of a higher power or find it difficult to derive comfort and guidance from religious rituals. The emotional burden of loneliness may overshadow their ability to fully engage with spiritual teachings and traditions.[8]

Moreover, the absence of social connections and a supportive religious community can impede the development of one's spiritual or religious identity. Studies emphasize that interpersonal connections within religious communities play a crucial role in shaping and nurturing spirituality. The lack of these connections due to loneliness can hinder exploration and growth, leaving individuals feeling adrift and detached.[9]

Writing in the *Los Angeles Times* just before the pandemic, Dr. Varun Soni, dean of religious life at USC, remarks,

> But over the last several years, these conversations have taken a devastating turn. Whereas students used to ask "How should I live?" they are now more likely to ask "Why should I live?" Where they used to talk about hope and meaning; now they grapple with hopelessness and meaninglessness. . . . What I have noticed in my work with students is that many of them face the same hidden root challenge: loneliness. . . . Students may have thousands of friends online, but few in real life; they may be experts at talking with their thumbs, but not so much with their tongues. As a result, many feel as though they don't have a tribe or a sense of belonging. *They feel disconnected from what it means to be human.*[10]

---

8. Richard M. Lee and Steven B. Robbins, "Measuring Belongingness: The Social Connectedness and the Social Assurance Scales," *Journal of Counseling Psychology* 42, no. 2 (1995): 232–41.

9. Chaeyoon Lim and Robert D. Putnam, "Religion, Social Networks, and Life Satisfaction," *American Sociological Review* 75, no. 6 (2010): 914–33.

10. Varun Soni, "Op-Ed: There's a Loneliness Crisis on College Campuses," *Los Angeles Times*, July 14, 2019, https://www.latimes.com/opinion/op-ed/la-oe-soni-campus-student-loneliness-20190714-story.html (emphasis added).

Addressing loneliness is thus not only about improving mental health but also about sustaining faith development and ensuring that individuals feel that they are part of a larger purpose. As such, ministries are uniquely positioned to create inclusive communities that can bridge the gap of loneliness, offering spaces for connection, conversation, and the shared pursuit of spiritual growth. By doing so, they affirm the intrinsic value of each individual and strengthen the collective fabric of spiritual life.

The Importance of Religious Community

Historically, the relationship between connectedness and spirituality has run in both directions. Loneliness affects the ability of people to be spiritually and religiously connected, but it can be mitigated by a strong religious community, especially for young people who often lack stability in their lives due to the chaotic nature of being a teenager.[11]

Religious communities have traditionally served as one of the primary points of connection for people, what sociologists refer to as "agents of socialization." In this way, they provide not only guidance for how to act and behave in social situations but also critical training grounds and safe spaces for young people to learn social skills inside a community.

When it comes to loneliness, the role of spiritual and religious well-being cannot be overlooked. Individuals who have a strong sense of spirituality or engage in religious practices tend to experience lower levels of loneliness because these communities provide a sense of meaning, purpose, and belonging in life, which acts as a powerful buffer against feelings of isolation.

As we've seen, studies have also shown that individuals who actively participate in religious or spiritual communities often benefit from a built-in support network. These communities foster social

---

11. Christine Comaford, "The Neuroscience of Loneliness—and 12 Proven Cures," *Forbes*, November 4, 2023, https://www.forbes.com/sites/christinecomaford/2023/11/04/the-neuroscience-of-loneliness-and-12-proven-cures/.

connections, encourage shared values, and provide a sense of belonging and acceptance. Moreover, spiritual practices like prayer, meditation, and attendance at religious services offer solace, comfort, and a source of strength during difficult times, reducing feelings of loneliness and promoting emotional well-being.

Aside from this functional purpose, religious communities also play an expressive role. Religion requires the practice of community to exist. The presence of others with similar beliefs, questions, practices, teachers, and sacred texts strengthens our own religious identity and commitment. Religion is fundamentally a communal exercise, and we need one another to sustain encounters with the divine.

Furthermore, spiritual and religious beliefs can help individuals make sense of their experiences, find purpose in adversity, and cultivate a sense of interconnectedness with others and the world around them. This broader perspective and connection to something greater than oneself can alleviate feelings of isolation and provide a sense of deep fulfillment.

While spiritual and religious health may not be a universal solution for loneliness, the research suggests that it can play a significant role in mitigating its effects. In fact, when looking across all their research, Gallup consistently finds that people who are religious and spiritual are better off in nearly all aspects of health, including social connection.[12] By nurturing one's spiritual well-being, exploring personal beliefs, and engaging with supportive communities, individuals find solace, meaning, and connection, which contribute to a sense of belonging and alleviate the pangs of loneliness.

Thus, social isolation among young people has a tremendous impact on their spiritual health. Not only are lonely young people disconnected from a fundamental sense of what it means to be human, as Dr. Soni points out, but they miss out on the

---

12. Bailee Blankemeier and Ilana Ron Levey, "Religion and Spirituality: Tools for Better Wellbeing?," *Gallup Blog*, October 10, 2023, https://news.gallup.com/opinion/gallup/512216/religion-spirituality-tools-better-wellbeing.aspx.

communities that can show them how to navigate these tough times by connecting them to a higher power.

They need to belong, and they need a belief system that contributes to their understanding of what it means to be fully human.

Belonging Precedes Believing

Unfortunately, we've completely misunderstood the direction of the relationship between belonging and believing. Religious leaders often take the approach that belief is the pathway to community, operating under the assumption that shared values and common faith will automatically generate communal bonds. They envision that once individuals accept certain doctrines or principles, a sense of community will naturally emerge. However, this top-down approach overlooks a fundamental aspect of human psychology and social behavior.

Sociologists and psychologists have consistently confirmed that belonging precedes believing. Émile Durkheim, one of the founding figures of sociology, emphasized in his seminal work, *The Elementary Forms of Religious Life*, that the primary function of religion is to foster social cohesion and solidarity.[13] He argued that it's the collective rituals and the sense of belonging to a group that give rise to shared beliefs, not the other way around. The communal experience creates a collective conscience—a shared set of beliefs and values that guide behavior.

Moreover, contemporary research supports this notion. Baumeister and Leary's "belongingness hypothesis" posits that humans have an intrinsic drive to form and maintain strong, stable interpersonal relationships.[14] They argue that the need to belong is a fundamental human motivation, influencing emotions, cognition, and behavior. When individuals feel a sense of belonging

---

13. Émile Durkheim, *The Elementary Forms of Religious Life*, trans. Karen E. Fields (Free Press, 1995).

14. R. F. Baumeister and M. R. Leary, "The Need to Belong: Desire for Interpersonal Attachments as a Fundamental Human Motivation," *Psychological Bulletin* 117, no. 3 (1995): 497–529, https://doi.org/10.1037/0033-2909.117.3.497.

to a group, they are more likely to adopt the group's beliefs and norms. This is further supported by social identity theory, which suggests that a person's self-concept is derived from perceived membership in social groups. The stronger the identification with the group, the more likely individuals are to internalize the group's values and beliefs.[15]

If we truly aim to instill long-term, durable beliefs and values among young people, we need to ensure those young people are embedded in a community that supports and connects them first. Adolescents, in particular, are navigating Erik Erikson's "identity versus role confusion" stage of psychosocial development, referenced in chapter 2, when a person seeks to establish their own identity and sense of self. During this critical period, a supportive community provides the necessary environment for positive identity formation. Research in developmental psychology indicates that adolescents are especially sensitive to social belongingness, and lack thereof can lead to negative outcomes like anxiety, depression, or susceptibility to adverse peer influences.

Belonging is the bedrock of religious formation. It's the foundation that will help a young person's faith withstand the inevitable winds and weight of being a teenager. Otherwise, it's like building a skyscraper without first drilling down to bedrock to set the pilings. It might look impressive initially, but the first gust of wind will send it tumbling to the ground—if it ever even supports its own weight in the first place. Just as a skyscraper requires a solid foundation to withstand environmental stresses, so too does a young person's faith require the foundational support of a nurturing community.

Consider the myriad challenges they might face: friends turn on them, a date stands them up, they don't get into the school they desire, or they find themselves alone in a new city for college or a job. Family upheavals, such as relocating for health or

---

15. H. Tajfel, "Social Psychology of Intergroup Relations," *Annual Review of Psychology* 33 (February 1982): 1–39, https://doi.org/10.1146/annurev.ps.33.020182.000245.

employment reasons, add additional layers of stress. In these moments of vulnerability, it's the feeling that they're not alone—that they belong to something bigger than themselves—that will keep them engaged in their faith.

Maslow's hierarchy of needs also underscores the importance of belongingness. Positioned right after physiological and safety needs, love and belonging are fundamental for psychological health.[16] Without satisfying these needs, individuals struggle to progress toward self-actualization and fulfillment. In a religious context, if young people don't feel they belong, they're unlikely to embrace the beliefs and practices promoted by the community.

As we see from the research above, belonging is the key to making so many of the things we want for young people possible. It's not enough to teach doctrines or expect that belief alone will foster community. We must actively create inclusive environments where young people feel seen, heard, and valued. By prioritizing belonging, we lay the groundwork for them to develop genuine, lasting beliefs.

Therefore, religious communities should reevaluate their approaches. Instead of focusing solely on doctrinal instruction, they should invest in building strong relationships and fostering a sense of community. Mentorship programs, group activities, and open discussions can help cultivate this environment. By doing these things, we not only support their spiritual growth but also contribute to their overall well-being. In other words, fostering a sense of belonging is, or should be, the primary concern of anyone who is concerned about the spiritual and religious beliefs of young people.

Selection Bias

It's a common oversight in ministry to prioritize belief, hoping belonging will naturally ensue. Many in ministry focus on belief first, influenced by the strength faith holds in their own lives—a faith so resilient it might withstand solitude in a cave. However,

---

16. Abraham H. Maslow, *Motivation and Personality* (Harper & Brothers, 1954).

those deeply involved in ministry, like readers of this book, don't often mirror the spiritual life of the average person. Your engagement with this material already sets you apart from those who may not prioritize such readings in their spiritual life.

This discrepancy is what social scientists term "selection bias"—drawing insights from a nontypical segment that doesn't accurately reflect the wider society. It's a reminder that ministers' deep-seated beliefs, shaped by unique experiences and choices, may not align with the general public's faith journey. This bias can lead to the false assumption that pathways that bolster one's faith journey are universally applicable.

For most, however, belief isn't sufficient on its own. A sense of community is essential; it validates and sustains one's faith. Belonging acts as the stabilizing force amid life's tumult, giving context and community to personal beliefs. Especially for youth, during life's trials and transitions, the reassurance that they are part of something greater than themselves is crucial. It is this belonging that maintains their spiritual engagement and fortifies their faith.

Delayed Gratification

Another reason why this equation is so hard to keep straight in our heads is that the immediacy of progress on the belief side can often be so much greater than progress on the belonging side in the short run. I mentioned in chapter 2 that I was once a counselor at a religious camp. I've seen firsthand how easy it is to create an experience that results in young people making firm and earnest commitments to faith. I can clearly remember leading young campers to a religious encounter with results so predictable that the whole experience became almost formulaic. It was thrilling in the moment to think that I had something to do with their transformation.

But I also saw how fleeting those commitments were when the young people weren't surrounded by a great community. Over time, even the most intense mountaintop experience will fade. The short-term win is often replaced by long-term disappointment.

On the other side, creating belonging is really hard at first. Helping someone become a part of a community to get them established with connections and people who care about them is slow going. You have to get people to break down their walls and overcome their fears. While I was really well trained in the belief side of things as a counselor, it took a while for me to develop a set of equally effective tools for building community among my groups of campers.

Investments in belonging tend to pay off momentously over time, though, when their networks, once small, begin to expand rapidly. I think about it like the social version of compound interest. For a while it seems like not much is happening, but steady investments return enormously in the long run. Getting invited to one thing with a couple of people turns into introductions to whole groups full of connections. Network expansion occurs exponentially, but it takes time.

Chasing belief first is like a firework. The explosion is often immediate, amazing, and awe-inspiring. If you've ever led a kid to a spiritual breakthrough, you know the rush.

Going for belonging first is like starting a snowball down the hill. It's so small at first and likely to break apart a million times before it catches on. It seems hopeless if the conditions aren't exactly right. You wonder if anything you did during the day made a real impact.

But you know where these analogies end. The firework will quickly fade into the sky as embers fall to the ground, requiring a new fuse to be lit and new energy to be expended just to maintain the experience. Meanwhile, the snowball will eventually gather momentum and get bigger and bigger.

How to Create Belonging That Leads to Belief

To create a sense of belonging that can lead to believing, religious leaders and trusted adults must engage young people as individuals and use the low-trust tools around relationships outlined in chapter 3. However, religious organizations must also do their part to help create a sense of belonging that extends beyond the individual and connects people to a shared sense of purpose and spiritual identity.

The pursuit of belonging can serve as a guide for religious organizations to strengthen their sense of community, maintain their traditions, and ensure that members feel a deep sense of belonging within the faith community. We often think that concepts like community and belonging are too amorphous to be guided. But the reality is that we can pursue some pretty clear actions to direct and build community, create belonging, and connect young people to a faith community in a way that also meets one of their biggest needs.

Charles Vogl has an MDiv from Yale and has spent his professional life focusing on how modern organizations can tap into cultural and religious lessons going back thousands of years to help build community. His book *The Art of Community: Seven Principles for Belonging* explores how to create and nurture strong and meaningful communities.

Vogl outlines seven key principles: boundary, initiation, rituals, temple, stories, shared values, and inner rings. Through these principles, he provides guidance on how to build communities that foster a deep sense of belonging, connection, and shared identity among members.

Congregations and ministries would do well to adopt those principles and use them as a guide for building places and spaces where young people can encounter one another and people who care about them in a way that leads to a stronger, more durable faith life. Let's take a look at each of those principles and how they can apply to religious organizations.

Boundary. In a religious context, the boundary represents the distinction between those who are members of the religious community and those who are not. It's important to create an environment where members feel safe to express their beliefs and values while also being open to outreach and inclusion of newcomers or those exploring the faith. However, there should be clear definitions for what it means to be *in* the group as opposed to *out* of it.

Keep in mind, though, that there can be different layers to membership, and not everyone needs to agree on everything to enter into the group. See the inner rings principle below.

Initiation. Initiation rituals and activities in religious organizations can include baptism, confirmation, or other ceremonies that mark a person's entry into the faith community. These rituals are significant moments that reinforce a sense of belonging and commitment. Some of these are sacramental in religious organizations, but others are based simply on local tradition.

Rituals. Religious organizations are rich in rituals, which can include worship services, holidays, and sacraments. These rituals have deep meaning and are essential for members to connect with their faith and with one another. Our rituals often fail to keep pace with the changing world and need to be updated more frequently than people think. For example, with more and more young people delaying marriage, there is now a sizable time gap between confirmation or high school graduation, which many congregations celebrate, and wedding rituals. It is important for religious organizations to build rituals surrounding that important time in life to keep people engaged.

Temple. The concept of a temple in religious contexts can be seen as a sacred place where the community gathers for worship, reflection, and connection with the divine. Creating and maintaining physical or spiritual spaces for communal activities is crucial. However, we shouldn't think that a temple can be *only* a physical space. We can have special spaces set aside online as well.

Stories. Religious organizations often emphasize the importance of sharing and passing down sacred stories, scriptures, and teachings. These stories help members understand their faith's values and beliefs and provide a shared narrative that binds the community together.

Shared values. Members of a religious community are typically united by a common set of values and beliefs. Clearly defining and reinforcing these values helps members understand who is part of the faith community and what that community stands for. It's important to remember, though, that coming to a shared set of values and beliefs is a process. It's often not linear, and it cannot be assumed forever just because of a onetime commitment.

Inner rings. Within religious organizations, there may be inner circles or leaders that play a crucial role in guiding and nurturing the community. These inner circles should uphold the values and traditions of the faith while also welcoming and supporting newcomers. Sociologists often refer to people having "careers" inside of organizations. This simply means that there are multiple pathways that people take to participate through a variety of roles over time. Organizations that do a good job of building community allow people to move in and out of different roles as they grow and mature with the organization.

An approach that combines personal relationships with the institutional structures identified above can facilitate the kind of belonging that leads to believing. Earlier in the chapter we saw how young people are retreating into isolation, and we know from the research presented earlier in this book that young people are not likely to trust institutions alone to pull them out of that retreat. They need trusted adults to take an approach rooted in relational authority, but they also need institutions to help connect them to real community where they can feel valued and welcomed.

This is how we get the equation right. This two-pronged approach that combines the personal and the institutional is how we create belonging that truly leads to believing.

CREATING COMMUNITY:
A Step-by-Step Guide for Youth Ministers

Introduction

Belonging ignites hope and drives belief. In chapter 4 we saw how belonging precedes believing and how connection to a spiritual community can counteract loneliness. Young people crave safe, familiar spaces where their presence and stories are valued. They find solace in community rituals and settings that replicate the camaraderie of a friendly, welcoming environment.

    Asking young people about their spiritual lives is key to building trust and a sense of belonging. They don't define belonging by exclusion but by the acceptance and resonance that they feel within a group. You can gather insights on belonging through qualitative research, laying the groundwork that reflects the spiritual needs of your community. This becomes a blueprint for guiding them in their faith.

    This chapter underscores that belonging is a precursor to belief. The codesign exercise outlined here allows young people to craft an online community that mirrors their values, fostering ownership and participation. Involving them in creating such spaces nurtures their faith in a community they shape, preparing fertile ground for their beliefs to grow.

Objectives

- Engage young people in the codesign of an online community.
- Uncover and articulate the shared values that underpin a sense of belonging.
- Facilitate a comparison between their ideal community values and those experienced in their current community settings.
- Provide a platform for presenting community insights to church leadership.

Pre-Activity Preparations

Materials Needed

- Flip charts or large whiteboards
- Markers of various colors
- Sticky notes in multiple colors
- Digital device with presentation software (optional)
- Projector or screen (if digital presentation is desired)
- Notebooks or journals for personal reflection

Setup

- Arrange the room so that flip charts / whiteboards are accessible to small groups.
- Set up a central area for group discussions and presentations.

Step 1: Envisioning Our Community (*Imago Dei*)

In step 1, participants engage in discerning the essential values and norms that define their ideal online community. This process is rooted in the belief that by critiquing existing online spaces and imagining new ones, young people can create a shared vision that fosters a deeper sense of belonging and engagement in their spiritual and communal life. The exercise underscores the importance of active participation in shaping environments that resonate with their values and experiences.

Introduction (Ten Minutes)

Explain the purpose of the exercise: to design an ideal online community to uncover shared values. Guide a discussion about what current online communities (e.g., Discord, Facebook, TikTok) look and feel like. What values are present in those? What do the participants like or dislike?

Community Brainstorming (Twenty Minutes)

Each group brainstorms what its ideal online community looks like, discussing the community's purpose, norms, and activities.

Step 2: Values Identification (Alignment)

Step 2 is a reflective exercise where participants delve into the core principles that they wish to see embodied within their community. By discussion and then a visual representation of these values, the activity encourages a deeper understanding and commitment to the ideals the participants want their community to stand for, emphasizing the role of shared values in cultivating a strong, cohesive group identity.

- Have participants discuss within their groups the core values that their community upholds and why these are important.
- Groups should then create visual representations of their community, integrating the identified values.

Next, focus on bridging the gap between the ideal and the real by comparing the values envisioned for an online community with those found in actual community groups. This comparison facilitates critical thinking about the congruence and disparity between participants' aspirational spaces and their real-life experiences in various social settings, fostering an awareness that can inspire practical applications and improvements in their existing communities.

- Have groups present their communities to one another, noting the key values they land on.
- Have a discussion as a group about how the values present in the communities compare to those in their in-person communities (religious, school, sports, work), noting similarities and differences.

Step 3: Presentation and Reflection (Pattern Recognition)

Step 3 involves synthesizing the collective insights on community values into a coherent message for church leaders, highlighting changes that could deepen young people's sense of belonging. The act of preparing and delivering a presentation is a crucial step for young individuals to voice their needs and suggestions, ensuring that their perspectives contribute to shaping a more inclusive and resonant spiritual community.

- As a whole group, consolidate the key values and principles that emerge.
- Prepare a presentation for church leadership, focusing on changes that would enhance young people's sense of belonging.
- Present the consolidated values and suggestions to the church leadership. You can do this in person or record the presentation on a phone to send to adult leaders.

Step 4: Extending Relationships (Scaling Up, Out, and Down)

"Extending and scaling" is the practical application of the workshop, where community insights are translated into concrete actions. It focuses on empowering adults to contribute to a welcoming environment for youth by identifying specific steps to promote belonging, thereby reinforcing a culture of active participation and shared responsibility within the community.

- Scaling up: Collect the values and ideas from the group discussions and synthesize them into a list of actionable insights. Use

these to guide future planning, ensuring that the ideals young people identify become part of the broader spiritual community.
- Scaling out: Share the ideas with other groups or leadership teams. Encourage them to apply these insights in fostering greater participation and belonging, particularly across different age groups or demographics within the community.
- Scaling down: Pay attention to individuals who may have expressed feelings of disconnect or unmet needs in their current communities. Reach out to these individuals for one-on-one or small-group follow-up, creating opportunities for deeper conversations about how to make belonging more real for them.

Conclusion

This facilitation guide outlines a structured approach to engaging young people in a collaborative process that mirrors the codesign practices prominent in design science. By involving them in creating an imaginary online community, the exercise allows youth to actively contribute to the cultural and relational framework of their church community. The resulting dialogue with church leadership provides a platform for their voices to be heard and their values to be acknowledged and acted on, enhancing their sense of belonging and investment in their faith community.

THE COVID EFFECT

What business are you in? This is one of my favorite questions to ask people when doing consulting of any kind. It turns out that people often think they're in one kind of business, but their actual day-to-day activities tell a different story.

In one of the early episodes of his *Trailblazers* podcast, Walter Isaacson interviewed Robert Harris, a music writer and broadcaster, about the collapse of the traditional music business when streaming and downloading became available. Harris had this incredibly enlightening thing to say: "So if you would ask record executives, what business are you in? they would have said, 'We're in the music business. Our job is to find musicians, record them, and present them to the public.' That's not true because they were in the physical thing business. That was the business they were actually in. They didn't realize it. And the proof of that is that the moment you could get music without having to buy a physical thing, their business collapsed, completely collapsed."[1]

The day-to-day activity that consumed them was not really all that well aligned with their actual mission as a company, and

---

1. Walter Isaacson, host, *Trailblazers*, podcast, season 1, episode 8, "Music: The Sound of Disruption," Apple Podcasts, July 5, 2017, https://podcasts.apple.com/us/podcast/music-the-sound-of-disruption/id1212045046?i=1000389536730.

Mr. Harris points this out so clearly. Many of us who are of a certain age can remember a time when we used to buy CDs or even tapes. When was the last time you did that? But you probably aren't listening to *less* music. It's just that you consume it differently.

Even though you aren't in a business in the traditional sense, I think you can see the parallels. Ask yourself, What business am I in? *How well does your answer align with the way you spend most of your time?*

Many leaders who work with young people, especially in ministry, found themselves forced to reconcile these two things because of the pandemic. If you asked them what business they were in, they would have told you that they connected with young people, brought them to Jesus, and facilitated their salvation and lifelong commitment to the faith. But that's often not how they spend most of their time.

The moment their ability to gather people together in a physical location went away, many of their ministries utterly collapsed, to use Mr. Harris's phrase. As it turns out, they were actually in the gathering or small events business.

That's not a bad business to be in or a bad skill set to have, but it's also not *necessarily* aligned with their mission.

A Tale of Two Ministries

In the early days of the pandemic, I watched many youth ministers and campus pastors struggle, and the most common question I heard was, "What do I do now that we can't get together like we used to?" Some entire church bodies shut down their youth ministry programs on the logic that youth ministry happens at the church building, and if we can't get together, then there's no ability or need to do youth ministry. I wish I were making that up.

But one group stood out in particular. Although they had a thriving on-site ministry with hundreds of kids coming each week, their leadership was clear that the business they were in wasn't about gathering young people.

In the very early days of the pandemic, they pivoted to meeting for prayer on FaceTime, dropping off care packages at people's doorsteps, helping young people make care packages for others, playing video games together, and organizing virtual study groups and thousands and thousands and thousands of text messages to check in, share Bible verses, and connect young people to one another. They even organized "missions" trips by teaming together to help a random low-ranking player win in the popular video game *Fortnite*.

They were able to pivot so quickly because they knew exactly what business they were in. Part of the reason they had this clarity in the first place was a key decision by leadership. Although the leadership had always tracked traditional metrics like attendance, these measures were used primarily for forecasting and planning, not as measures of success. They helped to answer questions about where more staff were needed or if they should pursue more and bigger spaces.

The more important metrics they used were relational. Their staff conversations were always about the spiritual progress of individual kids they worked with, as opposed to coordinating logistics and resources. These metrics served as the basis for their conversations and tactical shifts on a day-to-day basis.

When the pandemic hit, these metrics stayed right in place. The attendance numbers were down, which told them they probably didn't need a new building, of course, but their relational metrics continued to provide focus and progress on what mattered most to them: fostering relationships between young people and Jesus.

When they asked themselves the key question above about the alignment between time spent and organizational mission, they found that the two were consistently in lockstep with each other.

Contrast that with a friend of mine who has been in some form of youth ministry since we were in college together in the late 1990s. We talk often, and a few years ago he told me something I'll never forget. He said, "You know, most of my job at this point seems to be just driving around. I'm either shuttling kids, things, or things for kids to one place or another." It was an exaggeration, but I knew what he meant. His job had become almost entirely logistics to keep his program running. Some of this was his own creation, but much of it was put on him by the expectations of a congregation under the justification of "We've always done it this way." My friend doesn't work in youth ministry anymore. He got his degree in counseling and works in public schools so he can spend more time working with kids.

As we emerge from the pandemic, long-term pivots need to take place in terms of how we engage with young people, and it's critical that we understand the unique impact that COVID-19 has had on them. Nearly everything has changed at least a little bit for them, but some changes are more important. In particular, the way they think about faith and engage with institutional religion has been fundamentally altered. Additionally, the mental health of young people, already on shaky ground before the pandemic, has only worsened. Finally, the significant loss of learned social skills has been dramatic.

Each of these issues presents a challenge and an opportunity for those of us in ministry. They require us to pivot to be effective. And one thing is abundantly clear already: These pivots will only be possible if you and your leadership have absolute clarity about your mission and the business you're in and if you're willing to change the way you've always done things to pursue your mission.

Faith Is Moving

The pandemic was a disruptive force in the world of religion. In-person worship services were paused for at least a period of time in most places until restrictions eased or services could be made available virtually. Bible studies, youth gatherings, service events and trips, and much of the rest of the surrounding communal life of the congregation were also put on hold and had to be reconstructed with new safety requirements or rebuilt entirely from the ground up. Perhaps the biggest disruption was the loss of institutional knowledge and history as core leaders and volunteers moved on.

Among all this turbulence, the trends of a softening of American commitment to institutional religion marched on. According to Pew the rate of religious attendance by Americans continued its decline during the pandemic, and a 2022 PRRI poll shows that only 16 percent of Americans say that religion is the *most* important thing in their life.[2] Much of this was expected because it was largely the trend we were already on, even if there had not been a pandemic.

However, the greatest change in belief, identity, and practice during the pandemic was with young people. Where other age cohorts continued on their previous trends or even leveled off during the pandemic on key metrics, young adults experienced an acceleration. For example, in the 2022 American Religious Benchmark Survey the youngest group's participation rates declined the most.[3] Nearly 30 percent of them reported going to church less often after the pandemic. Additionally, young people's beliefs in what Gallup calls the "five religious entities" (God, angels, heaven, hell, and the devil) are the lowest of any generation. To take just one data point, only 59 percent of the youngest age group (eighteen-to-twenty-four-year-olds) believe in God.[4] Finally, a 2023 poll by

TABLE 5.1

Percent of US Adults Who Say They Attend Religious Services Monthly or More

	2019	2022
All US Adults	33%	30%
Christian	49%	43%
Ages 18–29	24%	20%
Ages 30–49	32%	28%
Ages 50–64	35%	32%
Age 65+	44%	41%

See "How the Pandemic Has Affected Attendance at U.S. Religious Services," Pew Research Center, March 28, 2023, https://www.pewresearch.org/religion/2023/03/28/how-the-pandemic-has-affected-attendance-at-u-s-religious-services/.

---

2. Jason DeRose, "The Importance of Religion in the Lives of Americans Is Shrinking," NPR, May 16, 2023, https://www.npr.org/2023/05/16/1176206568/less-important-religion-in-lives-of-americans-shrinking-report.

3. Lindsey Witt-Swanson, Jennifer Benz, and Daniel A. Cox, "Faith After the Pandemic: How COVID-19 Changed American Religion," Survey Center on American Life, January 5, 2023, https://www.americansurveycenter.org/research/faith-after-the-pandemic-how-covid-19-changed-american-religion/.

4. Megan Brenan, "Belief in Five Spiritual Entities Edges Down to New Lows," Gallup, July 20, 2023, https://news.gallup.com/poll/508886/belief-five-spiritual-entities-edges-down-new-lows.aspx.

The Wall Street Journal and NORC found that only 31 percent of younger Americans claim religion is very important to them, the lowest of all the age groups they surveyed.[5]

Additionally, the *way* people are worshiping has certainly changed. Although it hasn't been overwhelming, there is a decided uptick in Americans attending worship services virtually.[6] It's impossible to deny the convenience, safety, and other factors that make virtual attendance appealing as a part of many people's religious lives. In my own house, for example, we certainly don't want our son to attend confirmation classes solely online, but it's nice to have that option if we're out of town for a week. And when I was a professor, well before the pandemic, I saw this with my own students. They preferred in-person classes by a large margin, but with life, work, and other things to balance, very few of them got through a degree without at least some online classes. Now, of course, many students even work remotely.

In other words, it looks like we've got a generation of young people and parents who have come to expect an online option as part of the approach to religious attendance and education in the same way that they expect it in other parts of their lives.

These altered attendance patterns and habits have come along, unsurprisingly, with a change in the way young people are thinking about their faith and spirituality. While the pandemic might have altered traditional patterns of faith expression for health and safety reasons, it did not diminish the fundamental human need to engage with the transcendent. It did, however, offer up a much wider range of possible understandings of the transcendent and ways to engage the divine. In other words, the Christian concept of God is now just one of multiple options young people view as available to them.

---

5. Aaron Zitner, "America Pulls Back from Values That Once Defined It, WSJ-NORC Poll Finds," *Wall Street Journal*, March 27, 2023, https://www.wsj.com/articles/americans-pull-back-from-values-that-once-defined-u-s-wsj-norc-poll-finds-df8534cd?mod=article_inline.

6. Witt-Swanson et al., "Faith After the Pandemic."

While some recent polling suggests that young people are still strongly interested in spirituality and faith-related concepts, this has come mostly at the expense of institutional religion. Where young people once would have expressed high rates of belief in "God," they are now more likely to say they believe in a higher power.

This trend was in place long before the pandemic, but it was certainly accelerated by the disruption to traditional routines. The authors of the 2022 American Religious Benchmark Survey note that "the decline of religious attendance and the stability of religious identity over the past two years suggest a decoupling of identity and experience. Increasingly, religious affiliation may tell us less about the full range of religious and spiritual experiences Americans have and the extent of their theological commitments."[7]

The shifting landscape of faith among young people underscores a critical juncture in religious experience: the move toward personalization over institutionalization. As the notion of spirituality takes a more individualistic form, religious leaders and communities face the challenge of redefining their roles in a landscape where attendance no longer equates to religious commitment.

This evolution calls for a new paradigm in which religious institutions must navigate the delicate balance between fostering traditional communal worship and accommodating the growing desire for a more personalized spiritual journey. To remain relevant and resonant, faith communities may need to find innovative ways to engage with the rich tapestry of individual belief systems that young people bring without necessarily expecting increased pews as a measure of their spiritual influence.

The Grammar of Faith

While there are a multitude of ways to experience and express faith and spirituality outside of institutional religious expressions and traditional worship services, religious leaders are right to be

---

7. Witt-Swanson et al., "Faith After the Pandemic."

concerned about the numbers above. The lack of attendance, belief, and affiliation means, in part, that we've got a generation of young people growing up without the basic "grammar" of institutional faith.

Increasingly, young people don't have any idea what goes on behind the doors of a house of worship. They can't even imagine what the inside of a church looks like other than what they may have seen in movies or at the occasional wedding or Christmas service.

This presents obvious problems for those institutions and congregations themselves, but the implications are even broader. Think about how reluctant you would be to enter a space where you had very little or no understanding of what would happen once you entered or even how the building was laid out. Nobody likes to feel stupid or confused.

If you need help imagining what this is like, just talk to nearly any first-generation college student about their first weeks on campus. If their experiences were like mine and many of my students, you will hear stories about how intimidating it was and how many of them thought about leaving or never even coming in the first place.

A lack of familiarity with these spaces combined with the existence of insiders who take for granted that everyone already knows the basics about what happens at church is a recipe for people to feel like outsiders who don't belong in the exclusive club. Given that mix of variables, no reasonable person would expect strangers to just wander through the doors of a church.

The lasting impact of COVID has yet to be written, but the early trends for religious involvement suggest that young people, in particular, are not going to "spring back" to the habits and routines of previous generations. While there will always be a need to belong and believe, the expressions of faith and the sources they look toward as the authority for spiritual development are likely to be much more diverse.

Pastors, parents, and teachers need to understand that the default position of institutionalized religion in young people's lives has likely changed for the foreseeable future. Any effective engagement will need to be focused on long-term relationships that don't rely on a baseline of experiences or knowledge as a barrier to entry.

Time Is Paramount

Because young people are losing the grammar of institutional faith, we need to rethink many of our standard approaches for engaging young people. I've already covered the need to shift to more relational approaches, but we also need to rethink some of the other "containers" of ministry in light of the broader shifts in society.

The single biggest implication for all these changes probably has to do with our timelines for engaging with young people around issues of faith and belief. Where we used to let institutions drive those timelines in the form of school calendars, confirmation schedules, or Sunday school hours, for example, those containers of time no longer make any sense to young people as a way to hold faith and spiritual matters. For young people and parents who have little knowledge and experience of how the institutional church works and operates, those old schedules will not mean much to them and are likely to be seen as symbols of institutional power rather than the relational approaches they need.

The disconnection between institutional timelines and the younger generation stems from a fundamental shift in how those generations perceive and interact with time itself. In the digital age, where information flows rapidly and connections span continents in seconds, young people are accustomed to instant gratification and customization. They're not just digital natives; they are temporal natives too. Their world is one of on-demand streaming, personalized playlists, and content tailored to their specific preferences.

In contrast, the rigid schedules of institutional faith can feel like a straitjacket. Young individuals often see these schedules as relics of a bygone era, remnants of a time when information and experiences were less accessible. To them, these structures seem arbitrary and disconnected from their daily lives, creating a chasm between institutional faith and their reality.

To bridge this gap and reestablish a meaningful connection with young people, we must embrace flexible and responsive approaches to engaging with matters of faith and belief. This means breaking free from the confines of institutional timelines and being attuned to the rhythms of the younger generations.

> They're not just digital natives; they are temporal natives too. Their world is one of on-demand streaming, personalized playlists, and content tailored to their specific preferences.

Furthermore, each young person's journey is unique—whether we like it or not—and they may arrive at their own understanding of faith at different times and through various experiences. Therefore, we must be patient and flexible in our approach, understanding that faith development is a lifelong process.

Young people losing the grammar of institutional faith necessitates a reimagining of our engagement strategies with young people. The shift in timelines is emblematic of a broader cultural transformation, and to effectively connect with the younger generation, we must shed the rigid structures of the past. By embracing flexibility, fostering meaningful relationships, and harnessing technology, we can create a more inclusive and relevant space for young people to explore and deepen their faith and beliefs at their own pace and on their own terms. It's not a departure from tradition; it's an evolution that honors the timeless essence of faith in a rapidly changing world.

Mental Health Impact

Of course, the pandemic didn't affect just the religious behaviors and beliefs of young people. One of the most important impacts has been on youth mental health. There is no need to recite the litany of alarming statistics in this area. You've likely read the headlines and seen the reports calling youth mental health an "emergency" or an "epidemic" in its own right. In fact, the Centers for Disease Control and Prevention has noted mental health as one of the most important things facing youth today.[8]

On the one hand, it's probably not your job or in your training to deal with a young person who is experiencing a mental health crisis. They need professional help from licensed experts. But, on the other hand, what is perhaps most concerning about this crisis is that the rise is not just in acute mental health episodes.

The number of young people expressing relatively low-lying mental health challenges is also on the rise and comes with astonishing consequences and implications. So while you may not be a licensed mental health professional, it's likely that if you truly understand the business you're in, you have an important role to play in fostering the overall mental health of young people so that they can see and experience the work of God in their own lives.

Multiple studies confirm that the relationship between mental and spiritual health is what researchers call "bidirectional." This means that each one influences and affects the other. Spiritual health is strengthened by good mental health and vice versa.

This relationship has been well established by researchers in multiple disciplines over a long period of time.[9] In 2022, Gallup summed up their decades of research on the topic and noted that their most recent data support the "long line of studies confirming the connection between religion and wellbeing—making it one of the more researched and robust findings in all of the sociology of religion."[10] While we might often see religion as separate

---

8. Centers for Disease Control and Prevention, *Youth Risk Behavior Survey Data Summary and Trends Report: For Dietary, Physical Activity, and Sleep Behaviors; 2013–2023*, US Department of Health and Human Services, 2025, https://www.cdc.gov/yrbs/dstr/dietary-physical-sleep-behaviors.html.

9. Harold G. Koenig, "Religion, Spirituality, and Health: The Research and Clinical Implications," *ISRN Psychiatry* 2012 (December 16, 2012), https://doi.org/10.5402/2012/278730.

10. Frank Newport, "Religion and Wellbeing in the U.S.: Update," Gallup, February 4, 2022, https://news.gallup.com/opinion/polling-matters/389510/religion-wellbeing-update.aspx.

from mental health, we should not. If the business that we're in is one of supporting the religious and spiritual flourishing of young people, then we *must* pay attention to their mental health. While we need to leave the clinical diagnoses and treatments to licensed professionals, there are things we can do to support the overall mental health of young people and foster a stronger relationship with God.

Religious professionals and communities are uniquely positioned to draw from the lessons of their faith to play a crucial role in supporting the mental health and flourishing of young people, which will also strengthen their faith lives. Below are five of the central things we can do that will reinforce the unique relationship between faith and mental health:

1. Model and teach empathy and compassion. Empathy and compassion are key tenets of Christianity, and social scientists and mental health professionals emphasize the importance of empathy and compassion in fostering positive relationships and mental health. Unfortunately, many young people are not aware of the centrality of compassion to Christian religious teachings. We should model these behaviors in our interactions with others and teach them explicitly during religious instruction. This can help young people develop positive emotional skills and improve their relationships with others.

2. Provide support during life transitions. Adolescence and young adulthood are times of significant change and resulting stress. As adults, our lives tend to be much more stable, and it's easy to forget how disruptive major life changes can be. For teenagers and young people, change is constant. Religious professionals can provide support during these times, such as offering rites-of-passage ceremonies, providing counseling, or simply being a listening ear.

3. Encourage volunteerism and altruism. A core tenet of Christian religious tradition is an emphasis on the

importance of helping others. Encouraging young people to engage in volunteerism and altruistic behaviors can provide them with a sense of purpose and satisfaction, which is linked to improved mental health and well-being.
4. Bridge the gap between faith and mental health. There can sometimes be a stigma around mental health within religious communities. Religious professionals can help break down this stigma by openly discussing mental health, encouraging people to seek help when needed, and integrating mental health support into their services. They can work closely with mental health professionals and refer young people to these resources when necessary.
5. Teach coping mechanisms. Meditation, prayer, liturgy, and structured reflection have all been shown to act as coping mechanisms during times of stress. Teaching young people these practices can equip them with tools to manage stress and promote mental health.

The pandemic has forced mental health to the forefront of issues we must attend to in young people's lives. Religious leaders, pastors, educators, and parents, along with mental health professionals, have an important role to play in fostering good mental health. At the same time, the tools and strategies that promote positive mental health also lead to more flourishing religious communities.

Social Skills Gap

An additional pivot we need to make due to the pandemic concerns social skills. The biggest challenge to the social life of any group is not when things are hard or difficult. In fact, humans, including young adults and teenagers, are great at meeting challenges. We're remarkably resilient. The hardest thing is actually when roles are unclear or when people are unsure about what they're supposed to be doing and how they're supposed to behave in a given situation.

Role clarity, a pivotal concept in sociology, is essential for social stability, integration, and effective functioning in groups. It encompasses individuals' understanding of their roles and those of others, reducing conflict and confusion, promoting adherence to societal norms, enhancing group cohesion, and aiding in times of social change. It serves as a cornerstone for social order, ensuring that individuals connect with others who share similar roles, ultimately contributing to the harmonious functioning of communities and organizations.

A lack of role clarity induces stress because it plunges individuals into a state of uncertainty and confusion about their responsibilities, rights, and expectations within a given context. When individuals are unsure of their roles, they experience anxiety and frustration as they grapple with the ambiguity surrounding their duties and interactions with others. This stress arises from the inability to perform effectively, the fear of making mistakes, and the strain of navigating social situations without a clear road map, all of which can lead to reduced job satisfaction, emotional turmoil, and diminished overall well-being.

The lack of role clarity becomes particularly stressful when linked to the loss of social skills, which was experienced by young people during the pandemic when they were often unable to engage in their typical social activities. As the pandemic disrupted traditional social roles and limited face-to-face interactions, young individuals, in particular, found themselves thrust into a world where the boundaries of their roles became less defined. The stress derived from this ambiguity was compounded by the isolation and diminished social exposure, which hindered the development of crucial social skills. This combination of role ambiguity and reduced social engagement amplified stress levels, making it challenging for young people to adapt to changing societal dynamics and maintain a sense of belonging and well-being.

This loss of social skills and role clarity was one of the hidden costs of the pandemic for young people, and it promises to have lasting impacts. Despite calling them social "skills," we have the misconception that things like the ability to make eye contact, shake hands, and hold a conversation with someone you just met are personality traits. The lack of social skills often gets interpreted as a personality flaw rather than as a learned behavior, just like math, science, or art.

Some of us received explicit instruction in this area when we were young. I can clearly remember practicing shaking hands and standing up straight while I introduced myself over and over to my parents in our kitchen so that I would know how to do it in real life. Like many parents, my wife and I constantly talk to our son about dressing in a way that is appropriate for the place we're going.

For others, the instruction is more implicit, and perhaps more consequential. I also distinctly recall the laughter from peers when I showed up at school with my hair uncombed and the time I forgot a change of clothes and had to sit the rest of the school day after gym in my sweaty shirt and shorts. Those were less pleasant lessons, but I never forgot them. Sociologists refer to this kind of knowledge as cultural capital. The pandemic cost us a lot of cultural capital.

How to Do

Much of the way we learn about how to interact in social settings comes from being thrust into real-life situations and then having to immediately navigate them using whatever cultural capital we have. For all the practice we did in the kitchen, it took me a while to have the confidence as a young teenager to smile, shake hands, make eye contact, and ask someone how they were doing. It wasn't because I didn't care about the other person. It's just that knowing *what* to do isn't the same as knowing *how* to do. In other words, I needed the real-life experience.

When we try out new things in a social situation, we are rewarded with immediate feedback. Our cultural capital gets put to the test, and we watch how others respond. If the feedback is positive and you get praised, then you know to continue doing those things. If people laugh or ignore you, then it's probably going to make you think twice about behaving that way in the future.

Essentially, all these interactions help provide role clarity. With every piece of information, we learn a little bit more about what is expected of us in a given situation. When this works at its best, we learn the skills we need as the people around us come to expect more from us. For example, we don't ask thirteen-year-olds to have high-stakes personal interactions with college admissions counselors or potential employers. Instead, we guide them through age-appropriate stages.

Just as my parents helped me learn how to shake hands in the kitchen years before I started meeting people important to me as an adult, my wife and I help our son draft emails for his teachers that are respectful and clear long before he'll be writing communications as part of his job. I can't even imagine what the world would be like if my son and his friends were just dropped into the middle of a workplace with their current ability to write and communicate.

But that's more or less what COVID did for millions of young people. The pandemic essentially robbed young people of a couple of years of practice and development at a crucial time in their lives. Right when young people would normally have been venturing out into the world on their own, they were kept from moving around and interacting. Even as the world slowly opened back up, the social norms around distancing took a lot longer to change.

Those microinteractions with the clerk at the grocery store, navigating crowded hallways at school, ordering food at a restaurant, or being with your parent while they bump into a friend at the coffee shop and having to behave yourself during the most boring adult conversation ever or risk the wrath of your mother when you get in the car (I may be speaking from personal experience!) were all gone.

None of those moments is important on their own, but collectively they add up to thousands of small opportunities to learn and refine how to behave in person.

We often fail to acknowledge the impact of loss and adjust our expectations accordingly. Instead, we expect young people to engage with us and the world as if the pandemic never occurred.

This is akin to expecting my thirteen-year-old son and his friends to write all my professional emails—a formula bound to disappoint. Not only are we dissatisfied with the outcomes, but the young people are too. They sense they're not meeting the social interaction benchmarks set by previous generations, yet they can't pinpoint the cause.

Fear and Avoidance

So what happens when people are unsure of themselves, their role, and how to interact with others? Do they thrust themselves headlong into a situation and risk being laughed at and ostracized? Most of us just disengage. We avoid those situations. Nobody wants to feel incompetent.

But that disengagement is not really ever about who a person is at their core. The ability to interact in public has nothing to do with a person's heart, values, or beliefs. This disengagement is because of a lack of skills, not a lack of concern or humanity.

As adults, we need to understand that when young people who came of age during the pandemic express a reticence to engage in public life, it's not because they don't care or don't want to. It's often because they don't know how.

Talk to any teacher or professor these days, and they'll tell you that it's like the students they have now, while just as smart as their previous students, are missing something. As one of my former colleagues recently told me, "It's like they just don't know how to be students in a real classroom with other real students. They don't know when to speak up, how to calm down, or when to take chances, question the professor, or do any of the normal stuff they used to do. We've had to really work on that, almost more than the material itself."

The loss of social skills experienced by young people during the pandemic has significantly contributed to their disinterest or reluctance to engage in conversations about or activities related to religion. When individuals, especially young ones, struggle with social interactions due to the disruption of their normal social roles and reduced opportunities for face-to-face engagement, they often develop social anxiety or discomfort in group settings.

This heightened social anxiety is augmented when we couple those feelings with highly abstract conversations about important issues, including discussions about faith, which often take place within group settings, such as congregations or youth groups. Young people may feel ill-equipped or anxious about participating in these interactions, causing them to withdraw or avoid religious conversations and activities altogether. This avoidance can be further exacerbated if they perceive religious gatherings as having rigid or unfamiliar social expectations, making them less willing or able to engage meaningfully.

Adults who work with young people and care about their religious education and development would do well to focus on providing role clarity to help them overcome the social anxiety caused, in part, by the lack of practice many of today's teenagers have. You can play a crucial part in helping young people overcome these challenges by being transparent about roles and expectations in a given circumstance, coaching young people about how to engage with their religious and spiritual selves, and not assuming knowledge until it's demonstrated.

I recognize that this is easier said than done, however. Much of the way that we want people to behave and act is built on assumptions or logic that is rarely challenged. As soon as we start to communicate these norms explicitly, we have to defend those assumptions. When my dad told me I needed a firm handshake, I found myself wondering *why* I needed to shake hands that way. I'm still not sure I have a good answer for that one.

For matters of faith and spirituality, you probably will need some good explanations rooted in values or meaningful traditions that speak to young people if you're going to be able to provide clear guidelines for how to act in a religious setting, ask important questions, or even explain the various rituals that guide worship behavior. Just know that the more clarity you're able to provide, the more you'll put young people at ease and empower them to see pathways of future interactions and engagement as opposed to retreat.

Conclusion

In chapter 1, I suggested that if we are ever going to truly get to the reconstruction phase in the pandemic disaster, it will be young people who lead us. One way or another, this is true. Time marches on, and youth grow up to be adults and take on leadership positions. The work you do with them right now, while they're still young, will help determine what they value. The more you can understand the unique impacts of the pandemic on their lives, the more you'll be able to help them heal and access the religious and spiritual parts of themselves they so desperately need.

In some ways, their lives are never going to return to normal. For young people who missed major milestones in life or lost years of socialization, the pandemic will forever affect the way they understand the world. There is a unique opportunity to meet young people with empathy in this situation and rebuild some trust with them by being the caring adult they need. After all, *this* is the business you're in. You didn't get into this to build massive programs and report numbers up the ladder. You're here to use your knowledge and experience to help young people see God even as they navigate their own challenges, and there is no more important work in the world.

TEXT TO CONNECT:
Leveraging Empathetic Analytics

Introduction

In a world increasingly marked by isolation and emotional struggles, especially among young people, the church is called to be a sanctuary not only for spiritual growth but also for mental well-being. The urgency of this task is ever more evident given the soaring concerns around youth mental health, amplified by the ramifications of the pandemic. While mental health care is a specialized field best left to the experts, the church—especially youth ministers—has a significant role to play in fostering emotional and spiritual wellness. In line with this mission, this four-week activity is designed to be a holistic approach to pastoral care, blending data-driven insights with empathetic, faith-based interactions.

At the core of this initiative are daily emoji check-ins—a simple yet powerful tool to gauge the emotional pulse of your young community. Through a single emoji, participants can quickly and effectively communicate their emotional state for the day, providing the youth minister with an immediate, albeit abbreviated, insight into their well-being. This acts as an initial touchpoint for the minister to monitor, connect, and offer timely support.

SACRED LISTENING TOOL

To supplement these daily glimpses and dig deeper, twice-weekly prompts invite more nuanced reflections on faith, life, and other areas of interest. These open a space for youth to consider questions of significance and allow the minister to better understand the various facets that make up their daily emotional states.

The activity's final phase is dedicated to data analysis and tailored follow-up. Here, the gathered data from the check-ins and prompts are not just tallied but translated into actionable insights. The youth minister can identify trends, spot potential red flags, and most importantly, offer highly personalized pastoral care based on these insights. This not only enhances the depth of individual relationships but creates a domino effect of trust and openness within the larger youth community.

Objectives

- Implement daily emoji check-ins to allow young individuals to communicate their emotional states, enabling youth ministers to quickly assess and respond to the youths' mental health needs.
- Introduce twice-weekly prompts for in-depth reflection, creating a structured opportunity for youth to explore and articulate their feelings and experiences related to faith and daily life.
- Analyze the data from emoji check-ins and reflective prompts to discern patterns and potential areas of concern, informing the pastoral care provided by youth ministers.
- Use the insights gained from the check-ins and reflections to foster a supportive and responsive church environment, building stronger connections and trust within the youth community.

Pre-Activity Preparation

Materials Needed

- A smartphone with a texting plan
- A computer with Excel or Google Sheets
- The phone numbers of your youth group members (gathered with appropriate permissions)

Setup
- Create a spreadsheet.
- Open Excel or Google Sheets and create a new spreadsheet. Label the columns "Name," "Date," "Emoji Status," "Color-Code," "Monday Prompt," and "Thursday Prompt."

Step 1: Text Introduction (*Imago Dei*)

Send an introductory text to your youth group members explaining the purpose of the activity and asking for their consent to participate.

Here's an example: "Hi all, this is [Youth Minister's Name]. I'd like to start a daily check-in via text to see how you're doing and connect on faith and life topics. We'll just try it out for four weeks. Are you in? 😊"

As members agree, add their names to the "Name" column in the spreadsheet.

Step 2: Daily Emoji Check-Ins (Alignment)

The daily emoji check-ins serve as the heartbeat of this four-week program, offering a quick but profoundly insightful glimpse into the emotional states of the youth involved. The purpose here isn't just to collect data; it's to open a window into the daily lives of young people, many of whom are navigating challenging emotional and spiritual terrains. In essence, these daily emoji check-ins are miniature acts of pastoral care, leveraging technology to maintain a caring presence in the lives of young people.

Each day, send out a text asking how they are doing. Here's an example: "Good morning! How are you feeling today? Reply with an emoji. Here's mine: 😊."

Step 3: Extending and Scaling (Pattern Recognition)

You can create a community-wide fabric of support that reaches beyond the walls of your own ministry by scaling this activity. You'll be playing a crucial role in fostering not just the spiritual well-being but also the mental health of a larger community of young people.

Track responses: As you receive emojis, record them in the "Emoji Status" column corresponding to each name and date. Make sure to record your own as well!

Color-coding: Use conditional formatting to color-code the "Emoji Status" on the basis of your predefined color scheme (e.g., red for not good, yellow for OK, green for good, and purple for other).

Once the check-ins and prompts have been recorded for a few weeks, take time to review the data for patterns. Look for trends, shifts in emotional responses, or potential red flags that may need more attention. Use these insights to offer tailored follow-up and personalized support.

Step 4: Extending Relationships (Scaling Up, Out, and Down)

To make this exercise more impactful, ensure that the data and relationships generated through the check-ins contribute to scaling relationships in three dimensions—up, out, and down.

- Scaling up: Review the trends across all participants to inform broader pastoral care strategies or youth ministry programming. For example, if you notice many participants are struggling with stress, you could plan a group discussion or activity focused on managing anxiety.
- Scaling out: Collaborate with other youth ministers, educators, or religious leaders to share the model and extend its impact to more young people. This could involve adopting the check-in process in other groups or using the insights gained here to address mental health and spiritual care across broader communities.
- Scaling down: Use the individual data to engage more personally with participants, particularly those who may need additional support or care. Offer one-on-one meetings or smaller-group conversations to go deeper into their emotional and spiritual needs.

Conclusion

With this structured yet empathetic approach, you'll not only have tangible data but also build relationships that can have a lasting impact on the mental and spiritual well-being of your youth members. This methodology aligns with proven strategies to promote positive mental health and enhance religious communities. It models empathy, provides support during life transitions, and encourages reflection—core tenets that are grounded both in faith and in mental health research.

GROWING UP ONLINE

Emma

I've had the opportunity to present my work and research about young people hundreds of times over the years, and the presentations that always mean the most to me are the ones with young people in the audience or up on stage with me. I like to know if what I'm presenting passes the smell test with the people who are actually living the things I'm talking about.

At an event with young people in the audience a few years ago, the conversation turned toward the biggest, baddest bogeyman and scapegoat of all: social media. I'm not sure if I've ever gotten through the Q&A portion of a talk without this issue coming up. The questioners usually fall into two groups. The first consists of those who are genuinely confused and a little curious. Many adults in the church simply don't understand social media at all, especially the way teenagers engage with it. Hearing about the high rates of unhappiness, depression, and loneliness that young people themselves associate with social media usage, these adults will ask, Why don't they just delete those apps and turn off their phones then? It's an understandable question, even if it's a nearly impossible request.

The second group is less curious. They are pretty determined to believe that social media is the singular or at least predominant cause for the decline of the church, young people, and all society. Theirs is more of an emotional response. The logic works something like this: They didn't have social media when they were growing up, and they turned out just fine. This generation has social media and is moving away from God and the church. Therefore, social media must be the cause, and we should eradicate it. They will sometimes even couple this determination by citing statistics about the dangers of social media that someone posted in one of their Facebook groups. (I wish I were making this up.)

You've probably seen both camps. Maybe you find yourself leaning more toward one of them. But I think both approaches are misguided attempts to reconcile the role of social media and the internet in general in the lives of young people.

The result of either of these positions is often a form of retreatism from adults. They either don't understand social media, don't like it, or both, and so they simply don't engage. They don't have social accounts or only use them to publicize youth group or ministry events, not really engaging with young people. They don't ask young people about their online lives, and they haven't really tried to understand what, if anything, we should be doing to help guide young people in their use of these new technologies.

> "When adults dismiss my online life, they disqualify themselves from the conversation of my life."

After these two camps had said their piece and asked their questions at the event I mentioned above, a young person named Emma came to the microphone. She said one of the most profound things I've ever heard from a young person. It wasn't meant as a challenge, just a simple statement of fact. As the adults in the room argued about the world as it should be, this young woman simply stated the world as it actually was.

She said, "When adults dismiss my online life, they disqualify themselves from the conversation of my life."

IRL vs. IML

Essentially what Emma was saying is that there is no difference between online life and offline life. It's all just life. There is a popular acronym that you may have seen used on social media: IRL. "IRL" stands for "in real life." It started out as a way to distinguish between something you did or saw on social media and something that happened offline. For example, someone might post a picture of themselves with their best friend they hadn't seen in a while with the caption "Me and Chad IRL" to indicate that they were with their friend Chad in person.

For those of us who didn't grow up with the internet or social media, we think this distinction is important and useful to make. But if you talk to young people or watch how they use this term on social, you'll see that it's often used sarcastically. Emma approached me after the event was over and expanded what she said, telling me, "Adults want to make this big distinction between online and IRL, but they don't get it. There *isn't* an IRL. I like to just call it 'IML': in *my* life. That can happen on my phone, in person, or anywhere. I don't really see the difference, you know?"

The boundaries between online and IRL are not nearly as distinct and clear for young adults as they might be for us. Teens move seamlessly between social interactions on apps and social interactions in person, often referring to one during the other or picking up threads from a conversation over text or something they see online when they get together in person.

Megan Bissell, the architect of the Sacred Listening tools at the end of each chapter, has often remarked, "My kids talk to one another and their friends in memes." The static images or short videos that populate the internet and social media channels form the basis for a kind of shared language even when they're sitting across from one another.

For months after Emma made her comments, I would test her ideas with other young people. They were unanimous in their agreement with her. There simply isn't one "real" life and one "online" life. If we want to truly attend to young people, understand

> If we want to truly attend to young people, understand them, and have some degree of influence, we need to stop trying to figure out whether social media is good or bad and spend more time trying to figure out what our role can and should be to help them navigate these spaces that are new to all of us.

them, and have some degree of influence, we need to stop trying to figure out whether social media is good or bad and spend more time trying to figure out what our role can and should be to help them navigate these spaces that are new to all of us.

Benefits and Harms

In 2023, the office of the US Surgeon General issued an advisory about social media use among teenagers. Importantly, it notes that there are distinct benefits as well as harms that young people encounter online. Rather than simply categorizing social media as good or bad, the report encourages us to pay special attention to these new technologies because of the unique developmental stage that teenagers are in. The advisory is worth quoting at length here:

> Adolescents, ages 10 to 19, are undergoing a highly sensitive period of brain development. This is a period when risk-taking behaviors reach their peak, when well-being experiences the greatest fluctuations, and when mental health challenges such as depression typically emerge. Furthermore, in early adolescence, when identities and sense of self-worth are forming, brain development is especially susceptible to social pressures, peer opinions, and peer comparison. Frequent social media use may be associated with distinct changes in the developing brain in the amygdala (important for emotional learning and behavior) and the prefrontal cortex (important for impulse control, emotional regulation, and moderating

social behavior), and could increase sensitivity to social rewards and punishments. . . . *Because adolescence is a vulnerable period of brain development, social media exposure during this period warrants additional scrutiny.*[1]

For their part, young people will tell you more or less the same thing about social media. When asked about whether social media is positive or negative, they are quick to point out that it goes both ways. They recognize their dependence on it, and many would like to decrease their use, but it's also seen as an inextricable part of their lives.[2] Connections to family, friends, and issues they care about top the list of positives, while bullying, rumor spreading, and misinformation are the biggest negatives.

This understanding of social media as neither good nor bad reframes the way that adults in ministry positions should be engaging with young people online. We need to help them ask and answer fundamental questions, but online. What does God want from me on social media? How do I know if what I'm seeing is true? How should I treat others in this space? What can hold me accountable? As Becker reminds us in chapter 1 above, we should be thinking about the conditions rather than simple categorization.

Thankfully, I think we have, embedded in our theological and belief traditions, all the tools we need to help us in this regard. The ancient wisdom passed down from generations before us can help us guide and instruct new generations in new technology. Before we get to that, though, let's take a quick look at what the impact of all this new technology is on today's teenagers as a group of people. While I believe we have all the tools we need, it's important that we make sure to really understand what we're

1. Office of the Surgeon General, *Social Media and Youth Mental Health: The U.S. Surgeon General's Advisory*, US Department of Health and Human Services, last reviewed June 17, 2024, p. 5, https://www.hhs.gov/sites/default/files/sg-youth-mental-health-social-media-advisory.pdf (emphasis added).

2. Kim Parker and Ruth Igielnik, "On the Cusp of Adulthood and Facing an Uncertain Future: What We Know About Gen Z So Far," Pew Research Center, May 14, 2020, https://www.pewresearch.org/social-trends/2020/05/14/on-the-cusp-of-adulthood-and-facing-an-uncertain-future-what-we-know-about-gen-z-so-far-2/.

dealing with. Otherwise, as we have already seen, we run the risk of hammering away at a screw.

Growing Up Fast and Slow

We all know that Gens Z and Alpha are the first generations to have grown up with the internet, social media, and smartphones. While millennials might have been the first "digital natives," as they came of age when mobile and social technologies were first released, younger generations have lived their entire lives this way.

Critically, not only has this influenced young people's own habits and experiences, but they've been raised in many cases by parents who have been on devices since the first moments of their children's lives. Smartphones and posts to social media quite literally helped welcome them into the world as proud parents documented their first (and every) moments. Where the parents of millennials were often flummoxed by their kids' use of social media, parents of Gens Z and Alpha are rarely without their devices and indeed see them as much as parenting tools as anything else. These experiences of technology, as integrated into all parts of life since their very first memories, have shaped the lives of today's young people in unique ways.

I've been researching and giving talks about generations for a while now, and I think the best way to describe what is happening to Gen Z and Gen Alpha is that they're growing up fast and slow. This phrase captures the paradox of their development: While they are exposed to a vast amount of information and experiences online, they often lack the real-life experiences that previous generations had that helped them develop social skills, as we saw in the previous chapter.

This paradox is central to what often makes our experiences with teenagers today so confounding. On the one hand, they often seem to be reluctant or even incapable of the basic in-person interactions that we used to take for granted. At the same time, they also are more informed about what's going on in the world than nearly any other generation before them and most of the adults that I know.

I was testing out this idea with a young person in my own community while writing this book just to see if it resonated with him. James, fifteen, told me, "That's right. And we get it. We're not great at the in-person stuff. It's taking us longer to learn. But part of it is that I'm just so wary of listening to some adult tell me how to act when they can't even seem to understand that the world is, literally, on fire or understand even the basics of pronouns or why Russia's invasion of Ukraine is so important or a million other things that I see online every day."

His point here is important and contains a critical element of instruction for us. Just as Emma noted that adults disqualify themselves from the conversation of her life, James is showing us that when we ignore the things young people care about, we lose the credibility to speak into the other parts of their lives.

We don't have the time and space here to cover every aspect of digital and social media's impact on young people, but it is worth looking at one dynamic specifically. In what ways is technology contributing to a speeding up of traditional adolescent development, and in what ways is it slowing it down?

Growing Up Fast: Digitally Savvy and Globally Aware

Gen Zers are growing up fast due to their rapid adaptation to the digital age and their unparalleled access to information. In terms of their online exposure, Gen Z has access to a wealth of information and experiences that previous generations did not have. They are able to connect with people from all over the world, learn about different cultures and perspectives, and engage with a wide range of content. Credible studies routinely find that teenagers spend eight hours or more per day online.[3]

In other words, they are almost constantly connected. This exposure to a wide range of information and experiences has helped

---

3. Melinda Wenner Moyer, "Kids as Young as 8 Are Using Social Media More Than Ever, Study Finds," *New York Times*, March 24, 2022, https://www.nytimes.com/2022/03/24/well/family/child-social-media-use.html.

Gen Z develop a broad understanding of the world, which contributes significantly to their being one of the most well educated and politically informed generations.[4]

Technology is allowing for more exposure to diverse viewpoints and perspectives at younger ages than ever before. Young people aren't sitting around waiting for the morning paper or the five o'clock news. They get their information from a myriad of sources, including firsthand, personal accounts. Instead of having to spend years cultivating in-person relationships to get firsthand looks into others' lives and experiences, they simply open up their feed and find an array of people expressing opinions, sharing thoughts, and documenting their realities.

Growing up fast has four unique components for emerging generations:

1. Early exposure to information. Gen Z has grown up in an era of information abundance. With the internet at their fingertips, they have access to a wealth of knowledge, enabling them to learn about complex global issues, cultures, and perspectives from a young age. Research by the Pew Research Center indicates that 95 percent of teens in the United States have access to smartphones, providing them with a constant stream of information and connectivity.[5]
2. Digital literacy. Gen Z is exceptionally digitally literate. They have mastered navigating various digital platforms, from social media to online learning tools, and possess a keen understanding of online communication. Their ability to discern credible sources and engage in online discussions sets them apart from previous generations.

---

4. Samuel J. Abrams, "Gen Zers Are Anything but Politically Ill-Informed," American Enterprise Institute, April 30, 2021, https://www.aei.org/politics-and-public-opinion/gen-zers-are-anything-but-politically-ill-informed/.

5. Monica Anderson, Michelle Faverio, and Eugenie Park, "How Teens and Parents Approach Screen Time," Pew Research Center, March 11, 2024, https://www.pewresearch.org/wp-content/uploads/sites/20/2024/02/PI_2024.03.11_Teens-and-Screens_REPORT.pdf.

3. Global perspective. Unlike earlier generations, Gens Z and Alpha's exposure to diverse perspectives and cultures through the internet has made them more globally aware and open-minded. They are more likely to support social justice causes and advocate for inclusivity and equality. Not only are they demographically the most diverse generation in history, but their online lives are often even more diverse than their in-person interactions.
4. Entrepreneurial spirit. The digital age has empowered Gen Z to explore entrepreneurial endeavors at a young age. They are more likely to start their own businesses or engage in freelance work, leveraging their digital skills and global awareness. Various studies have highlighted the entrepreneurial spirit of Gen Z; a higher percentage of them express a desire to start their own businesses. This is indicative of their adaptability and ambition in the fast-paced digital landscape.[6]

Growing Up Slow: Delayed Social Skills and Milestones

The phrase "growing up slow" captures the idea that, in some aspects, Gen Z has been delayed in acquiring traditional social skills compared with previous generations. This delay can be attributed to several factors, many of which are intertwined with the rapid advancement of technology and some of which have also been covered in the previous chapter.

While Gen Z may know more about the world than previous generations of young people, their online lives can also expose them to negative content and experiences. For example, social media can be a source of cyberbullying, harassment, and other negative interactions. Additionally, the constant stream of information can be overwhelming and lead to anxiety and stress that

---

6. Mehrzad Saeedikiya, Aidin Salamzadeh, Yashar Salamzadeh, and Zeynab Aeeni, "Cognitions Affecting Innovation Among Generation Z Entrepreneurs: The External Enablement of Digital Infrastructure," *International Journal of Entrepreneurial Behavior & Research*, March 11, 2024, https://doi.org/10.1108/IJEBR-02-2023-0188.

both is real in its own consequences and also contributes to a reluctance to engage in in-person interactions, which are often seen as less controllable.

In chapter 4, I wrote about how the brain processes exclusion in the same way that it processes physical pain. Our experience of being left out of a group is more than just FOMO. It actually hurts us. Historically, this pain response served us well because we had no choice but to seek social interaction for survival. However, in the peculiar landscape of 2024, something unusual has occurred. While we are more connected than ever through our devices, we also have the power to disconnect abruptly. Amid the pain of social exclusion, individuals can choose to isolate themselves further, even though it goes against their nature as inherently social beings.

The result of this retreat is that, in contrast to their fast-paced online lives, Gen Z's real-life development can be slower in some ways. In addition to the lack of traditional social skills discussed above, younger generations seem to be reaching traditional markers of adulthood, such as finishing education and leaving home, later than previous generations.

They are also engaging in "adult" activities such as having sex, dating, drinking alcohol, going out without their parents, and driving much later than previous generations. Some theorists have suggested that a new developmental stage is needed to account for the fact that youth today are taking longer to reach adulthood and are more reliant on their parents than generations past.[7]

Generation Z's journey of growing up fast and slow encapsulates the complex interplay between their digital immersion and traditional social skill development. While they may lag in certain aspects, such as face-to-face communication, they excel in digital literacy and global awareness.

7. Katie Bishop, "Kids Getting Older Younger: Are Children Growing Up Too Fast?," *BBC*, March 24, 2022, https://www.bbc.com/worklife/article/20220324-kgoy-kids-getting-older-younger; Mike Males, "The Not-So-Rebellious Youth Revolution Coming to Your County," *Yes!*, June 6, 2023, https://www.yesmagazine.org/health-happiness/2023/06/06/youth-revolution.

Cognitive Dissonance

When people experience inconsistency between their beliefs and actions, they feel a sense of discomfort known as cognitive dissonance. This fundamental principle from psychology suggests that people will either change their behavior or adjust their beliefs to resolve this internal conflict. The cognitive dissonance that growing up fast and slow presents for young people is a conflict between competency and inadequacy. They feel competent in areas where they often see adults coming up short and feel inadequate in the places where those same adults excel.

Living in a long-term state of cognitive dissonance can come with dramatic mental health consequences and is not a state of being in which a person can thrive. This is why psychologists have noted that we move to resolve this conflict as soon as possible through either behavior or belief change.

Given that young people see their online presence as a necessary component of their lives as teenagers, you can imagine what they choose. It's easier to resolve the conflict by coming to the determination that the adults in your life simply aren't in touch with what you care about and don't really know you.

It's our job as adults to cross that gap, engage young people where they are, validate their experiences as important, and become a caring presence in their lives. If we can do this, then we can resolve the cognitive dissonance for them. They will no longer have to choose between thriving online and coming up short in person, because we will be there to help blur those boundaries with them.

New Technologies and Ancient Practices

The speed at which new technology is adopted matters not just because it's interesting but because it means that we've barely had time to keep up, if we're keeping up at all. As a culture, we typically guard against the harmful effects of change by developing social norms and standards that govern how we use new things. When adoption is relatively slow, we're able to put these norms in place in real time.

To use another example from the world of communication technology, my grandmother tells me stories of how she was expected to act and use the party-line telephone installed in her house. There were basic social norms for the good of the community that involved keeping the line open for emergencies, not eavesdropping, and clearly stating who you were and whom you were looking for. Of course, these norms were violated as norms always are, but that they were more or less agreed on and reflected community values meant that even when they broke down, there were opportunities to reinforce them through correction.

We are living through the process of developing those norms for social media right now. These platforms feel like chaos to anyone over the age of thirty partly because the rules of engagement are not yet clear. How do we treat one another in this space? Was that post passive aggressive or just sarcasm? Can we please get some punctuation to indicate the tone of voice? Is that what emojis are supposed to do? Should I "like" something that is sad just to show support for that person?

We are working out these and a million questions like them on a minute-by-minute basis. The way we answer them, as is always the case with emerging social norms, will ultimately be both guided by and reflective of our collective values.

If we take seriously the statements by Emma and James above, as well as the research, what we will find is a need for adults to help young people navigate a complex world where digital life is integrated into daily life.

The ministry question is then, How do we guide young people to engage with social media and other digital technologies in a way that strengthens their faith? I believe part of the answer can be found in the ancient Catholic concept of accompaniment.

Walk Alongside . . . Online

"Accompaniment" means to come alongside for a journey. Although the concept can be traced back hundreds of years, it has lately gained traction in Catholic communities after Pope Francis's emphasis on the importance of accompaniment in the context of pastoral care and outreach to younger generations. In *Christus Vivit* (2019), Pope Francis discusses the idea of accompaniment extensively.

His claim, essentially, is that young people need trusted adults who are willing to journey together with them through adolescence and faith exploration and development. The underlying premise is that being in ongoing relationships with others is sacred and spiritual work, not simply an evangelical tactic (though it is that as well).

As much as the concept of accompaniment involves being in a continued relationship with someone, it does not simply mean to journey together with no destination or end in mind. As Pope Francis himself writes, "Spiritual accompaniment must lead others ever closer to God. . . . To accompany them would be counterproductive if it became a sort of therapy supporting their self-absorption and ceased to be a pilgrimage with Christ to the Father."[8]

Although we don't have the room to dive fully into the concept of accompaniment, there are some key components that are worth considering as we think about what it might mean to journey with young people through their online and offline lives.

- Personal encounter. The church should walk alongside young people, showing them genuine care and understanding. Actual presence is critical. This approach helps them navigate the challenges and complexities of the modern world by providing them a constant and reliable touchstone.
- Listening and dialogue. Pope Francis emphasizes the importance of listening to young people, valuing their voices, and engaging in meaningful dialogue. This approach allows the church to understand young people's concerns, doubts, and aspirations.

---

8. Pope Francis, *Evangelii Gaudium: Apostolic Exhortation on the Proclamation of the Gospel in Today's World* (Vatican Publishing House, 2013).

- Faith formation. Formation along the journey is not simply saying and doing the right things, and it's not immediate or transactional. It's not just about conveying doctrines but about helping young people develop a deep and personal relationship with God so that their hearts and minds are gradually shaped and molded.
- Being a witness. Adults, including religious leaders, should serve as positive role models and witnesses of the faith. Their actions should reflect the teachings of Christ, making faith more appealing and relatable to younger generations.

Importantly, accompaniment does not simply mean hanging out with young people. While it calls us to be in a relationship with them, it doesn't ask us to be their friend. Much like the model of relational authority offered in chapter 3, true accompaniment requires adult expertise. When I think of what young people need from trusted adults to navigate their online lives, I can't think of a better or more fitting concept than accompaniment.

To accompany young people online, though, we need to dive in and understand these new technologies. You don't necessarily have to use them as much as young people do, and goodness knows you don't have to understand all the slang they use. (Who could keep up?) But church and ministry leaders cannot simply ignore social media or position it as ancillary to "real" life.

But how? How do we engage young people through a technology many of us weren't raised with and may only barely understand? How can we even begin to have meaningful and authentic engagements online when memes, trends, and challenges come

> When I think of what young people need from trusted adults to navigate their online lives, I can't think of a better or more fitting concept than accompaniment.

and go faster than we can keep up? Thankfully, I don't think we have to do much too different from what we've been doing for in-person interactions. We simply need to extend our efforts to include young people's online lives.

Analog Tools Online

One of my favorite questions to ask a young person is, What music are you listening to these days? I didn't come up with it. It was gifted to me by a youth minister friend. I think it's a perfect question to ask a teenager. In one short question you set yourself up as a listener, someone who is interested in something they deeply care about, someone who is curious and not always an expert, and someone who is willing to take the time to talk to them about something that most adults ignore. It's beautiful that way.

More often than not, this leads to both of us on our phones searching for different artists. Then, they watch, sometimes in awe, as I create a playlist on my phone with their name to store their recommendations. It gives me something to ask them about next time we meet or even text them about later. Like I said, it's a perfect question.

When I get really lucky, it can lead to a conversation about *why* they like that music, what the lyrics convey, and if the songs are reflective of their values or make them think about bigger questions. And of course, those are the conversations that I'm really after.

Lately, I've been taking the same approach to young people and social media. If I see them scrolling, especially on TikTok, I ask them simply, "Who do you follow?" It turns out to be a wildly personal question, as you can imagine, and it only really works if I am willing to share my own social feeds. As it turns out, I don't have to worry about revealing too much of myself, because my social feed is about as interesting as watching paint dry to your average teenager. In the short time I do share, though, I get to convey vulnerability and even occasionally get a little tech help.

The real magic comes when they share their feeds with me. Just as I do with the music, they get to watch me follow some of the influencers they care most about on my own feed, and I get to know a little bit more about them.

But here's the thing. I don't really like social media all that much. I personally find very, very little value in it. But I love knowing more about the young person across from me. I'll always be interested in that, so I'm here for it. I'll listen to them share all day about whom they follow, why, what it means to them, what it says about their values, if they've ever unfollowed or blocked someone, how they made that decision, and a myriad of other things. You see, every one of those decisions is a reflection of their personal values and beliefs. And those are the conversations I'm really after.

For their part, young people seem to increasingly crave these in-person interactions. They know that much of what they see online is not fully authentic. Our research studies with teenagers indicate this in a myriad of ways. Only 15 percent of teenagers tell us that they trust social media influencers, while 76 percent of them say they trust the people they have relationships with.[9] There does not seem to be an end to this mistrust of online interactions either. Over half of teenagers told us that they were growing skeptical of the things they see online because they don't know what is produced by artificial intelligence and what is produced by humans.

You've likely got your own go-to moves that open conversations and relationships with young people. My point in sharing the example above is not to say that every adult in the country should be running around accosting young people and demanding to know who they follow on Instagram. Rather, I want to make the point very clearly that we don't have to radically rethink everything that we do just because we're talking about social media.

It's not some great mystery. Once we realize that the lines between IRL and online life are essentially meaningless for today's teenagers, we begin to understand that the approaches we take to accompanying them in person are also what's needed to accompany them online.

---

9. Future of Faith, *Sacred Listening, Deeper Faith: A Research-Driven Approach* (Future of Faith, 2025), https://www.futureoffaith.org/sacredlisteningstudy.

Making *Minecraft* Better

When I got my first job out of graduate school, my wife and I quickly made friends with Mark and his wife. Mark was another young professor, but he and his wife were ahead of us by a few years in every way. They even had school-age kids already, which was unthinkable to my wife and me at the time. We were just starting to think about having kids, and our friends had three! We learned so much about parenting by watching them, and our own son has benefited in a myriad of ways that are impossible to fully account for. One thing in particular has always stuck with me.

One day, when I was sitting in Mark's office, his phone rang. It was a simple conversation with his oldest daughter about arranging some logistics for after-school transportation to practice. At the end, he said he loved her and told her, "Make your school a better place today." I asked him what he meant by that last part, and he told me that he and his wife believe that if you're a Christian or a person of faith, then everywhere you go should reflect that. School should be better because you go to school as a *Christian* student and treat people accordingly. The conversation I overheard was not the first time his daughter was hearing this, of course. It was simply a reminder.

I have carried that little piece of unintentional parenting advice with me ever since. I use it often when I drop my own son off at school. Increasingly, I find myself using it for things that are not in-person interactions. While we don't allow our son to have social media yet, he does talk with friends on Discord, via text, and while playing video games. Lately, I've been telling him to make sure that *Minecraft* is better off by his being there as he disappears into the basement for his allotted daily screen time.

We have dinner table conversations about what that means. We occasionally unpack his confirmation class lessons in terms of what it means for how he should act and behave when he's playing games with people or chatting in a gaming community. As much as he blurs the lines between his "real" life and his online life, we are trying to do the same. The message we're trying to convey to him is that his values and beliefs do not get switched off when the computer gets switched on. Our expectations for him and what God wants from him are not excluded from these online interactions.

To the extent that he identifies as Christian, or at least a Christian in formation, his interactions online should reflect it. This means we talk a lot about not only what he produces in terms of his own actions but also what he consumes online. What does each of these things say about a person? Are they in line with what he wants people to think about him and how he thinks about himself? In a very real way, we're trying to walk alongside him and accompany him in *his* world.

Conclusion

Young people today are growing up differently from any generation before them. The combination of growing up fast and slow makes for a day-to-day existence that can often leave young people feeling like they are ping-ponging around life with no clear markers or milestones.

The art of accompaniment Pope Francis talks about is powerful for just this situation because it provides a framework for how to think about our ongoing interactions with young people wherever they are. Young people need accompaniment online just as much as they have always needed it in the other parts of their lives. They need guides and guidance from people who know how to travel and navigate, even if they've never been down this exact path before.

SACRED LISTENING TOOL

BUILD MEANINGFUL RITUALS:
A Step-By-Step Guide to Embracing Technology in Youth Ministry

Introduction

Social media and digital spaces offer unique prospects for fostering healthy habits and spiritual growth among youth. Adults must guide young people through these platforms, encouraging informed decisions and balanced online practices to promote well-being. Incorporating science-backed habit formation, we recommend daily engagement with resources like prayer apps to deepen faith rituals.

Mentoring in the digital age means trusting youth to navigate online spaces responsibly, using them for positive self-expression and advocacy. It's not about judging but about supporting their authentic use of these tools for beneficial outcomes. This guidance aims for continuous involvement with these practices and extends community building beyond immediate circles. As facilitators, we should adapt our activities to suit the varying interests and needs of young individuals within our faith communities.

Virtual spaces and social media platforms offer a unique opportunity to nurture healthy rituals and habits that can positively affect the spiritual lives of young people. It's essential that we, as mentors and leaders, guide them in harnessing these tools for personal growth, community building, and faith formation.

Informed by habit-formation science and designed for a faith-based community, this activity revolves around the daily use of a prayer or meditation app. However, the guide is adaptable to other themes and platforms that resonate with you and your young people.

Objectives

- Encourage young people to make informed decisions about their digital habits, guiding them to use social media and technology as tools for positive self-expression and spiritual growth.
- Utilize digital resources, such as prayer and meditation apps, to establish and deepen daily faith rituals among the youth, fostering a consistent practice of spirituality.
- Leverage virtual spaces to extend the reach of community building, connecting young individuals within and beyond their immediate faith circles in meaningful ways.
- Tailor digital ministry activities to match the diverse interests and needs of young people, ensuring relevance and engagement in their faith journey.

Pre-Activity Preparations

Materials Needed

- Smartphones or computers for app installation
- A projector or screen to demonstrate app features
- Notebooks and pens for each participant to take notes and use as a journal
- A spreadsheet software (like Google Sheets) for tracking responses
- Handouts with daily reflection questions

Setup

- Research apps or platforms. Spend some time researching prayer, meditation, or other faith-based apps that you think would benefit your group. Alternatively, you could also use long-form readings or another form of engaging content. Suggested apps and websites for daily engagement include:
  - Hallow. This app offers guided Christian meditations, bedtime stories, and prayers. It covers a variety of themes, including humility, gratitude, and calmness.
  - Insight Timer. Though not specifically faith-based, Insight Timer has thousands of free meditations, including spiritual and religious practices.
  - Pray.com. This app offers daily prayers, Bible stories, and a community for shared prayers.
  - Our Bible App. Catering to a more progressive audience, this app offers various Bible translations and devotional readings.
  - YouVersion. This Bible app provides daily Bible verses and allows for in-app reflections and journaling.
- Create accounts. Before you introduce the app to your group, set up your account and explore its features so you can guide them effectively.
- Schedule reminders. For the first week, plan to send nudges or notifications to remind your young people to engage with the app.
- Draft weekly follow-up texts. Create text prompts for weekly follow-up and responses. An example prompt could be, "Write down five words that come to mind when you reflect on your daily app usage."

Step 1: Introduction and Purpose (*Imago Dei*)

Begin by discussing the power and risks of social media and virtual platforms. Establish that the purpose of this activity is to create meaningful rituals that enhance your group's faith journey and give them something affirming to do with their devices as a small way of beginning to reset their relationship with these technologies.

SACRED LISTENING TOOL

Guide participants through downloading the app, signing up, and navigating to the specific area they'll be engaging. Explain that this is a four-week commitment designed to take minimal daily time but offer substantial spiritual benefits. Show them how to set up reminders and notifications. Allow time for questions and ensure everyone is comfortable with the app's user interface and features.

Hand out a list of reflection questions that they should consider as they journal each day. Alternatively, some apps will have a journal feature built-in with questions that you can use. Some examples of daily reflection questions include

- What was the most challenging part of using the app today? What got in the way?
- Write down what popped into your mind as you were engaging with the app today.
- How did the content on the app resonate with your personal beliefs or goals?
- What would you share with someone close to you about your experience with the app today?

Step 2: Daily Routine and Weekly Check-Ins (Alignment)

Habit formation is rooted in the science of the habit loop, which involves a cue, a routine, and a reward, as elucidated by Charles Duhigg in *The Power of Habit*. Consistent cues (like a specific time of day or preceding action) can trigger a routine (such as praying). When followed by a rewarding experience (perhaps a sense of peace or accomplishment), the cycle reinforces the behavior into a habit. Neuroscientific research supports this, showing that through repetition neural pathways become more efficient at activating these patterns, essentially "wiring in" the habit. This is especially powerful when coupled with social or communal rewards. When you help young people in a group associate prayer with regular, specific cues and intrinsic rewards, they're more likely to develop these practices into enduring habits.

There are some important things to keep in mind as you lead the experience with the app that can help your young people build long-term habits.

- Daily engagement: Encourage the young people to choose a specific time each day to engage with the app.
- Reflection time: Each day after they engage with the app, have them reflect on their experience by journaling about the reflection questions.
- Weekly text prompts: Send out your prescheduled text prompts to foster discussion and reflection. Keep records of these in a spreadsheet, noting the date, initials, and their responses.

Example weekly text prompts:

- Week 1: Respond with five words that come up for you as you reflect on your week using the app.
- Week 2: Respond with one sentence about your favorite session this week.
- Week 3: Respond with five words that capture how you feel about your experience with the app so far.
- Week 4: Respond with one sentence that you would use to share your experience with someone close to you.

Step 3: Extending and Scaling (Pattern Recognition)

In this step, you're going to compile the responses from your weekly check-ins in a spreadsheet so you can see how individuals engaged with the activity over time. Look for patterns and commonalities in the data so you know how to follow up.

The purpose of this phase is to extend the impact of this meaningful practice beyond the youth group, inviting adults and other members of the community into the fold. The aim is to strengthen the social fabric of our community, promote intergenerational dialogue, and create a shared space for spiritual or intellectual growth. As adults join in, they don't just observe; they participate, reinforcing the idea that learning and growth are lifelong processes.

Convene a gathering with your young people and invite adults from the community. Make it clear to adults that their role is to listen. Facilitate a discussion among the young people about their experiences, challenges, and learnings in light of the data captured. Use this as an opportunity to celebrate their efforts and discuss next steps. Share insights and recommendations with the adults about how they can continue to support the young people in their faith journey.

Step 4: Extending Relationships (Scaling Up, Out, and Down)

- Scaling up: After collecting the insights from participants' daily reflections and weekly text prompts into a shared repository, like a spreadsheet, use this data to understand the broader trends in how young people are engaging with the app and forming habits. These insights can inform future programming or resources for youth ministry. You can also use this information to craft a group reflection or a larger community discussion about the use of digital tools for spiritual growth, ensuring that the impact of this exercise resonates beyond just the individual participants.
- Scaling out: Encourage the involvement of a wider range of participants by extending the activity to other groups within the community, including adults and leaders. By integrating other age groups and different sections of the faith community, you foster intergenerational dialogue around digital spiritual practices. This helps build a culture where both young people and adults use technology to reinforce their faith, promoting broader community engagement with the digital resources used in the exercise.
- Scaling down: Follow up individually with participants who may be struggling to establish consistent daily habits or who have shared more personal reflections about their experience with the app. Offer personalized guidance or additional resources to help them deepen their spiritual practice. You might also identify

those who express significant growth and encourage them to take on a mentoring role, helping others develop similar habits.

Conclusion

By thoughtfully integrating technology into our faith practices, we can forge a pathway for meaningful engagement and community building. This guide aims to be a flexible tool for encouraging lifelong spiritual habits in an ever-evolving digital landscape.

7

MICRONARRATIVES

In chapter 1 of this book, I mentioned that as a researcher, I always wanted to be seen as *useful* rather than *interesting*. This book has been an effort to take some seemingly disparate ideas and data points about young people, faith, and social dynamics and weave them together in a way that helps you, at a very practical level, attend to young people better and more effectively.

It is my sincere belief that with the right understanding and tools, such as the Sacred Listening tools described at the ends of the chapters, you can truly maximize your impact in the life of a young person and create a vibrant, flourishing faith life with them. In turn, we can also begin to revitalize our religious structures and institutions, many of which are staggering at the moment.

As we close, however, I want to leave you with a big idea about how to think about emerging generations in their historical contexts. I offer this not because I think it's particularly smart but because it provided a key insight for me personally that helped in my own work with young people and even with my own son. Sometimes, a change in thinking can be the most practical tool we have.

The Rise of Micronarrative

It is often said that we are living in a postmodern age where truth is constantly in question, and people reject singular explanations that hold the world together, such as the American dream or democracy, or even Christianity. In his 1979 book *The Postmodern Condition: A Report on Knowledge*, Jean-François Lyotard sums up postmodernity as "incredulity toward metanarratives" like political or religious systems.[1] What he means is that the postmodern era is one where people are increasingly skeptical of any singular source of knowledge or of any one worldview. The postmodern world is often characterized as one that is fragmented and chaotic with no source of objective truth.

Much of what is written in the chapters above might lead you to believe that we are living in the postmodern era right now. When we see young people treating faith as a conversation, relying on relationships for guidance where expertise is just one component, rejecting the authority of large social institutions, and needing a community of people who affirm their worth before they will begin to form long-lasting beliefs, it's easy to jump to the conclusion that young people are rejecting the notion of authority and truth altogether.

But I think this understanding of young people is fundamentally misguided, and it comes from not truly listening to teenagers or watching them carefully. When we take the time to stop and hear what young people are telling us about their world, we find a much different reality.

They are not embracing moral ambiguity and disregarding a cohesive worldview. This is not the death of the metanarrative. It's the rise of micronarrative. The micronarrative is the centering of self in an integrated life that includes everything from relationships to religion to retail and recreation and everything else.

They aren't rejecting the *concept* of an overarching narrative; they're rejecting institutional authority as the *source* of that

---

1. Jean-François Lyotard, *The Postmodern Condition: A Report on Knowledge*, trans. Geoff Bennington and Brian Massumi, 10th ed., Theory and History of Literature 10 (Manchester University Press, 1984), xxiv.

> The micronarrative is the centering of self in an integrated life that includes everything from relationships to religion to retail and recreation and everything else.

narrative. They see themselves as in the midst of constructing, or attempting to construct, an integrated and cohesive worldview with an integrity that can make sense of their political, economic, and social choices, as well as their fundamental human needs around things like faith and belonging. They see themselves as contributing members of the community.

What we perceive as fragmented and chaotic appears that way only because it's still very much a work in progress and not particularly centered on key social institutions. In this light, every young person is like a kind of nascent theologian or moral philosopher in training.

This shift in perspective changed everything for me. When I stopped thinking about young people as rejecting truth and began to understand them as people in pursuit of a truth they can live with, I was knocked out of my judgmental position and put back in my teacher role.

People who are trying to make sense of the world need guides and teachers. They need to work out ideas through writing, conversation, and art. Just like all other students, they need to learn through experiences and get feedback on those ideas from people they trust.

We know it's ineffective to teach writers by making them copy books word for word. At some point, probably very early on, we encourage artists to explore their own ideas in paint or clay or whatever their chosen medium is. Architects don't simply design the same buildings over and over again.

While some command of the basics is fundamental to mastering any new body of knowledge, good educators recognize that rote memorization and blind devotion to an institutional authority will never produce true learning.

When I began to take this perspective, that young people are simply in the middle of a messy process of making sense of the world and need trusted adults to be guides and teachers, all the various data points about young people and beliefs started to make sense to me. Only a group of people engaged in a sense-making process would continue to express high levels of belief and spiritual activity along with low levels of institutional trust, participation, and affiliation.

The micronarrative they are constructing isn't necessarily rooted in some subjective sense of the world beyond what you might normally expect from teenagers. I haven't run into much of what Robert Bellah and colleagues famously call "Sheilaism," which they use as a shorthand to describe one of their research respondents, Sheila, who crafted an entire religious system by listening to her "own little voice."[2]

Instead, with their micronarratives young people are trying to reconcile the wisdom of ancient traditions with modern realities. They're trying to figure out how to live in community with integrity and fidelity to core sets of belief. If you listen to young people, you'll hear them trying to figure out things like how they can care so much about the environment and still order so much stuff shipped in individual boxes from Amazon. I have had students sit in my office debating taking a job that pays more money so they can help their families versus pursuing their passion and purpose in life, or whether they can really be part of a campus ministry that excludes LGBTQ+ people and maintain their very diverse friendships with people they love.

I don't mean to paint a picture of the world where every fifteen-year-old that you come across is deep into some existential exploration at all times. Far from it. Most of the conversations I have with my own teenager are about all the things teenagers have ever

---

2. Robert N. Bellah, Richard Madsen, William M. Sullivan, Ann Swidler, and Steven M. Tipton, *Habits of the Heart: Individualism and Commitment in American Life* (University of California Press, 1985), 221.

cared about (sports, video games, school, peers, etc.). Teenagers are far more likely to want your attention to show you a YouTube video or TikTok than they are to ask you about the meaning of life.

But that doesn't mean they aren't *also* asking all the hard questions. The only real question is whether you'll get to hear the hard questions when they do ask them. The answer to that entirely relies on the perspective that you have about young people in relation to life's most fundamental concerns. Do you see young people as vessels that need to be filled up with the right information, or have you made the shift to realize that they're trying to construct a life that makes sense and holds up when it is actually examined or used? If you see them as empty vessels, you'll be far less open to the moments when they ask questions. If you see them, essentially, as students, you can lead with curiosity and the kind of relationships that lead to true, lasting connections.

The Stories *They* Tell Themselves

At the beginning of this book, I made the point that the stories we tell ourselves about emerging generations are not particularly helpful. Our stories are built on assumptions that are often untrue and wrapped up in our own experiences as young people that we try to map onto a different time and era. As we have seen throughout this book, young people today are clearly living with some very different challenges and realities that make it nearly impossible to use our own experiences as reliable guides.

In this book, I have tried to tell a different, more scientifically informed story about what is really going on with Generations Z and Alpha so that we might be able to do ministry in fresh ways that speak more directly to those generations and have a bigger impact.

In this last chapter, though, I think it's worth mentioning that just as we have been telling ourselves a story about young people that reflects our own biases and hasn't always been based in reality, young people are doing the same thing. They are telling themselves a story about *us*. And the stories they tell often end up reinforcing many of the narratives explored in the chapters above. They see adults as not really understanding them, as more concerned about the institutions and traditions they represent, and as out of touch and unwilling to listen.

The exercises and other action steps outlined in the chapters above are designed to help you know, understand, and respond to the young people in your community more effectively. They have another effect as well. As much as they will help you connect with young people better and break down some of the assumptions you might have about them, they are also intended to break down the assumptions that young people have about *you*.

If you can employ one or more of the Sacred Listening tools described here and on our website (www.futureoffaith.org), you'll find that you're systematically undoing the preconceived ideas that young people have about adults. The more you listen in structured ways, convey that listening, and take action based on what you've learned from young people, the harder it will be for them to maintain the narrative that adults don't care about them. It will be harder for them to feel alone. It will be more difficult for them to see you and other adults as untrustworthy. They will slowly come to see you as a safe person with whom they can try things out and make mistakes. If you can treat listening as a sacred exercise and duty, it will make it significantly harder and less desirable for young people to retreat into their personal bubbles.

In the introduction, I mentioned that you don't need a big national dataset or volumes of research to tell you what's most important. Instead, you need insight about the young person in your church, school, or community. You don't need to know what an anonymous data point in some city halfway across the country has to say. You need to know what's in the heart and mind of the student across the table from you.

Some of the ideas in the chapters above will help you understand more about what emerging generations are facing, but ultimately the sacred work of listening, writing things down, and following up in structured ways is up to you. The information and insights you most need can be provided only by you and your community.

Gathering that information and acting on it in ways that support young people directly is ministry in the twenty-first century.

There is nobody better positioned to do it than you. No expert, research firm, or scientist with fancy letters after their name can do the work that needs to be done to reach young people today. Only you can.

And really, that's always been the case. The only thing that has ever mattered in the faith life of a young person is the attention of a caring and trusted adult. That's more true now than ever. I know you have the heart to reach young people, and now you have some tools. I can't wait to hear the stories of your impact!

INDEX

accompaniment, 174
Ammerman, Nancy, 85, 87
artificial intelligence, 21, 178
authority, 5–6, 32, 92–93, 97–100, 105, 129, 144, 176, 190, 192

belonging, 5, 41–44, 49, 53–55, 78, 111, 119–29, 131–35, 150, 191
bias containers, 26
Bissell, Megan, ix, 11, 92, 165

Calcutta metaphor, 1–3, 6
caregivers, 70
categorization, generational, 19, 22, 26
civility, 24, 114
communication theory, 7–8
confirmation, 4–5, 65, 101, 128, 142, 145, 179
connectedness, 119–20
COVID-19 pandemic, 5, 21, 44–45, 111–12, 137, 140–41, 144, 152

data collection, local vs. national, 10, 12–15
demographics, generational, 14, 27, 135

digital culture
  and discipleship, 36, 62–63
  and diversity, 26–27, 29–32
  and Gen Z/Alpha, 19, 99
doubt, 7, 62, 65, 68, 77, 97, 119, 175

education, 30, 65–66, 85, 89, 115, 142, 154, 172
empathy, 9, 35, 56, 62–63, 95, 148, 155, 161
evangelism, 11, 175

faith formation, 5–6, 176, 182
forgiveness, 26, 96
Future of Faith, ix, 7, 11, 95, 178

Gen Alpha, 3–5, 19–21, 27–28, 31–32, 37, 43–44, 111–12, 168, 171, 193
Gen Z, 3–5, 19–21, 27–29, 31–32, 34, 37, 43–44, 82, 99, 111–12, 167–72, 193
Gilbert, Daniel, 24–25
grace, 26, 98
grief, 7, 46

high-trust tools, 88–89, 91

Index

identity, 32, 41, 43, 60, 62–63, 67, 69, 87, 119, 121, 123, 127, 133, 141, 143
imago Dei, 8, 52, 76, 106, 132, 159, 183
individualism, 192
in-group/out-group bias, 25
institutional trust, erosion of, 5, 90
intentionality, 7–8
intergenerational relationships, 51–52, 79, 185–86

listening, 6–14, 31–32, 53, 59–60, 64–65, 93–98, 105, 138, 148, 169, 175, 177, 190, 192, 194
love, 11, 26, 30, 42, 71, 87, 96, 115, 124, 178–79, 192
low-trust tools, 5, 49, 91, 103, 126

Mastroianni, Adam, 24–25
mental health, 5, 42, 44, 46–48, 111, 120, 140, 146–49, 157–61, 166–67, 173
micronarratives, 4, 6, 189–92
models, ministry, 3–8, 10–16, 20, 27, 32, 35–37, 47, 51, 55–56, 75, 78–79, 88, 91, 100–101, 103, 109, 124–25, 138–40, 145, 159–60, 164, 167, 174, 176, 181–82, 186, 192–93, 195
moral decline, 24
motivation, religious, 57, 59–62

narrative, power of, 10, 15, 189–91
negativity bias, 25

online life, 164–65, 178–79

parenting, 63, 88, 168, 179
pastoral care, 36, 157–60, 175
pattern recognition, 2–3, 9, 53–54, 78, 108, 134, 159, 185
political polarization, 21, 29
practices, faith, 70
presence, ministry of, 5, 11, 13, 115, 123

privacy, online, 165–66
programming, youth, 5–15, 57–58, 113

racial identity, 27, 32
relational authority, 5, 92–93, 97–100, 105, 129, 176
relational ministry, 13, 51, 75, 109
relationships, 6–11, 13–15, 22, 42, 44, 49, 52, 54–55, 78–79, 92, 95, 98–99, 100–103, 105–9, 113–14, 117, 122, 124, 126, 129, 134, 139, 145–46, 148, 158, 160–61, 170, 175, 178, 186, 190–91, 193
religiosity, 82–83, 86–88
resilience, 36, 42

Sacred Listening, ix, 6–14, 52–54, 77, 92, 95, 178
Sacred Listening tools, 6, 10–12, 14–15, 51, 75, 105, 131, 157, 165, 181, 189, 194
safety, emotional, 49, 95
scale, redefinition of, 14–15
scaling relationships, 7, 78, 103
science, social, 4, 10, 20, 38–39, 61, 83, 91, 112, 125, 148
Scripture, 15, 69, 128
secularism, 83, 86
self-efficacy, 7
silence, 9, 94, 107
social isolation, 113, 121
social media, 5–6, 9, 21, 30–31, 44, 47–49, 52, 99, 111, 163–71, 174, 176–79, 181–83

tools, Sacred Listening. *See* Sacred Listening tools
trust, 4–6, 8–11, 13, 16, 37–39, 47, 49, 55, 79, 84–85, 87–95, 97–100, 103, 105, 107, 108, 114, 118, 129, 131, 155, 158, 178, 191–92
Twenge, Jean, 21, 38

youth ministry, 15, 91, 100, 138–40, 160, 181, 186

www.ingramcontent.com/pod-product-compliance
Lightning Source LLC
Chambersburg PA
CBHW020939180426
43194CB00038B/407

"Josh Packard is one of the voices I trust most when it comes to the faith and life journeys of today's teenagers. His research is both profound and practical and gives us new lenses to see and appreciate the young people we care about most. If you care about the next generation, *Faithful Futures* is a must-read."

—**Kara Powell,** Fuller Seminary and Fuller Youth Institute

"*Faithful Futures* is absolutely essential reading for youth ministers, parents, senior pastors, and anyone else who cares about young people and faith. With grace, wisdom, and a welcome dollop of common sense, Packard reframes the research we've been (mis)reading about young people and religion and offers up a refreshingly readable and surprisingly useful book. (Pro tip: Don't skip the spot-on practical exercises from Packard's cofounder, Megan Bissell.) If you read only one book on youth ministry this year, this should be the one."

—**Kenda Creasy Dean,** Princeton Theological Seminary

"Packard has once again given us a thoughtful, research-driven resource that meets this moment. His deep understanding of Gen Z and Gen Alpha helps youth workers move from theory to faithful practice. What I value most is the hopeful vision he casts. These generations are full of promise, and this book equips us to engage them with wisdom and care. Anyone serious about reaching young people should study this work closely."

—**Jake Bland,** president/CEO, Youth for Christ USA

"Maybe since the dawn of modernity listening for the sacred has been a struggle. But even so, in this late modern moment it's particularly difficult. It is hard work. Trying to hold on to anything sacred inside technological advances, capitalist drives, and political struggles has been a hallmark of modernity itself. But most often modernity has given us an empty cacophony because the sacred has been drowned in subjectivity. The only way back to something sacred—into any form of the sacred—is to listen. Packard has given us an important way to listen to young people. And more, he's given us a way to help lead them into listening. This book is filled with insights on the challenges and importance of listening and how this listening can reconnect us with the sacred. This is a timely and important book. It will go right onto my syllabi."

—**Andrew Root**, Luther Seminary; author of
Evangelism in an Age of Despair

"In a season when it feels increasingly difficult to bridge cultural and generational differences, Packard offers readers hope, practical tools, simple solutions, timely insights, and more. *Faithful Futures* is more than a book that helps readers understand and appreciate the opportunities young people bring to our communities; it is a road map that provides clear pathways for creating spaces where people of every generation can fully belong."

—**Arthur L. Satterwhite III**, vice president of strategy, Young Life